A Practical Guide to SUCCESSFUL ESTATE PLANNING

Iowa • Minnesota • North Dakota • South Dakota • Wisconsin

A Practical Guide to SUCCESSFUL ESTATE PLANNING

Iowa • Minnesota • North Dakota • South Dakota • Wisconsin

MARK R. ALVIG, CFP
THOMAS M. PETRACEK, CFP

Estate planning is unique to each individual. This guide is intended as a starting point to provide general information. It is not intended to give any specific legal or tax advice. Every plan needs careful, personal analysis. When developing an estate plan, consult with a team of advisors, including your Attorney, CPA or Accountant, Financial Planner, Investment Advisor, Life Insurance Professional, and Property/Casualty Professional.

Wealth Enhancement Group, LLC
125 W. Lake Street
Wayzata, MN 55391
1-800-492-1222
www.wealthenhancement.com

ISBN 1-58007-021-3

For additional copies of this work, contact:
Specialty Press, 11605 Kost Dam Rd.
North Branch, MN 55056, 651-583-3239
800-895-4585

ABOUT THE AUTHORS

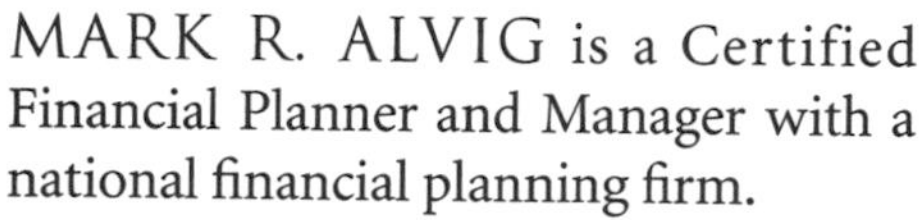

MARK R. ALVIG is a Certified Financial Planner and Manager with a national financial planning firm.

Since graduating in 1983 from Minnesota State University with concentrations in business, finance, and insurance, Mark has held financial planner and trainer positions with several national and regional financial planning firms. He has developed and presented many seminars on topics such as Estate Planning, Charitable Gift Planning, Retirement Planning, and Tax Reduction Strategies.

Mark, a Certified Financial Planner since 1989, co-authored the book What You Need To Know To Keep Your Farm in The Family. His experience in working one-on-one with hundreds of clients allows Mark to identify the necessary components to build an effective financial plan.

THOMAS M. PETRACEK, a Certified Financial Planner, is associated with Wealth Enhancement Group and a Registered Representative of FSC Securities Corporation. Wealth Enhancement Group is a team of financial professionals who provide comprehensive wealth management services with a focus on sound, diversified investment portfolios that are "tax efficient."

Tom graduated in 1976 from the University of Minnesota with high distinction, with a Bachelor of Science emphasizing Agriculture. Out of college, Tom owned and operated an agribusiness until 1986 when he transitioned into financial planning working with business owners throughout rural Minnesota.

In 1992, Tom earned the Certified Financial Planner (CFP) designation, and co-authored the book What You Need to Know to Keep Your Farm In The Family.

Over the past 10 years, Tom has developed and presented seminars focusing on Estate Planning, Senior Asset Preservation, Long-Term Care Issues, Reducing Your Tax Burden, The Roth IRA, and more.

Tom's business and financial planning experience, combined with his education, have provided him with the skills and knowledge to identify and develop a plan of action to put families' financial positions in order with confidence.

CONTRIBUTING EDITORS

SCOTT M. NELSON, a Minneapolis native, received his B.S. degree from St. John's University in Government and Accounting. Scott worked as an accountant at Arthur Anderson and Company in Minneapolis, auditing large and small companies in several industries. He then attended the University of Minnesota Law School and graduated magna cum laude in 1986.

While in private practice with the St. Louis Park law firm of Rossini, Nelson & Rossini, he developed his specialties in tax, business, and estate planning. Scott is a Competent Toastmaster and an officer of the Hennepin County Bar Association Tax Section, a former president of the Monday Tax Forum, a member of the Minneapolis Estate Planning Council, a class agent for St. John's University, and an Advisory Board member for North Hennepin Community College's Legal Assistant Program. He is also active in several professional and nonprofit groups.

Scott has published technical tax and accounting articles for the Minnesota Society of CPAs and teaches seminars on business and personal tax and estate planning.

DAVID HESS, a Registered Financial Consultant, is one of the cofounders of the Wealth Enhancement Group. Dedicated financial professionals, the Wealth Enhancement Group provides wealth management services with a focus on sound, diversified investment portfolios that are tax efficient.

Dave received a Bachelor of Science in Business from the University of Minnesota in 1969 and a Juris Doctorate from the University of Minnesota Law School in 1974.

At the beginning of his career, Dave

spent seven years with an international CPA firm in the tax area. He was an executive vice president with a local private banking and trust company until 1996 when he left to establish the Wealth Enhancement Group with his partners. Dave is an experienced estate and income tax planner, and has specialized in personal financial management for over twenty-five years.

Dave has frequently spoken to the Minnesota Bar Association, and the Minnesota Society of CPAs. He also taught estate and gift taxation in the Master's of Business Taxation program at the University of Minnesota.

Dave is a Registered Financial Consultant, a Certified Public Accountant, and an Attorney. He is a member of the International Association of Registered Financial Consultants, the American Institute of Certified Public Accountants, the Minnesota Society of CPAs, the Minnesota Bar Association, and is President of the Minnesota Chapter of the American Association of Attorney-Certified Public Accountants, Inc.

TABLE OF CONTENTS

Introduction: A Perspective on Estate Planning 1

1 Estate Planning: What Is It and Why Does It Matter to You? 3

2 Your Income Taxes and the Taxpayer Relief Act of 1997 5

3 Your Estate Taxes and the Taxpayer Relief Act of 1997 17

4 Wills and Other Ways 31

5 Planning For Liquidity 43

6 How to Use Trusts In Estate Planning 55

7 Getting More Out of Giving: Charities and Your Estate 69

8 Planning For Your Retirement 77

9 Medicare and Medicaid: What You Need to Know 87

10 Planning "Just in Case ..." 99

11 The Family-Owned Business: Structures, Strategies, and Succession 117

12 Ten Common Mistakes in Estate Planning 131

13 Glossary of Estate Planning Terms 133

14 Asset Inventory and Estate Planning Worksheet 143

INTRODUCTION

A Perspective on Estate Planning

Historically, estate planning has been perceived as a resource for the wealthy.

Today wealth is commonplace. Estate planning has become significantly more than writing a will. The aging of our society and increased life expectancies create more issues than just disposition of assets. Health, health care, asset preservation, asset management, business transfer, estate tax reduction, and probate avoidance, to name a few, are all issues of estate planning.

Estate planning is the most challenging area of financial planning. This book contains a list of ten common mistakes in estate planning because the majority of people who have started estate planning have made mistakes. Mistakes may cause families to have countless problems handling an estate. Some mistakes may cost heirs thousands of dollars or more.

The purpose of this book is to be a general guide designed to cover a broad range of essential estate planning topics. It is in a format that demystifies the topics and brings significant awareness of a wide range of issues that must be dealt with for effective, comprehensive estate planning.

Accomplishing an effective, well-thought-out estate plan is a challenging process. The techniques examined in *A Practical Guide to Successful Estate Planning* will help in making correct choices when beginning or continuing an estate planning journey.

Estate Planning: What Is It and Why Does It Matter To You?

"Estate planning." For most people, that term seems intimidating. That's why so many people put off doing something that would make life easier for themselves and for their loved ones. But estate planning really doesn't need to be intimidating. After all, since you plan for so many other things in life, it just makes good sense to put a little time and thought into this aspect of your life. It's well worth it.

What is an *estate?* In simple terms, it's everything that you own.

> ***Estate***—All your assets, including your home, real estate, bank accounts, securities, retirement plans, and insurance policies.

In English common law, the basis for our legal system, the term "estate" meant the land to which a person was lawfully entitled. The Old English term meant material condition or status. Today the term refers to anything that you own now and anything that you will potentially own in the future.

Estate planning involves all aspects of your life. It involves thinking about what can happen to you, to your health, and to your family. That means that you need to consider such matters as your assets and your debts, your needs and your interests as you grow older, and how you can best take care of yourself and the people close to you.

If you own a business, estate planning also involves ensuring that your business will be in good hands after you retire or when you die.

If you care about your family and everything that you've worked to acquire and to build, then estate planning should be important to you. There's a lot you need to do to ensure an independent future for yourself and a generous endowment for your loved ones.

Estate planning requires time and effort. What's involved?

- You need to make sure that you know what you own. This means taking inventory of your property and other assets.
- You need to know the facts about your ownership, to determine and document legal ownership.
- You may also need to retitle (change legal ownership), transfer, or sell certain assets.
- You need to identify beneficiaries and heirs and to determine how much and how soon they will receive their share of your estate, perhaps by setting up trusts.
- You need to make decisions about how to reduce the impact of estate taxes and how to fund for them to keep the

government from unnecessarily shrinking your estate.
- You need to prepare for health care.

These are the major areas involved in estate planning.

> ***Retitle***—To change the legal ownership (title) of property.
>
> ***Beneficiary***—Person who receives benefits from such assets as trusts, insurance policies, and estates.
>
> ***Heir***—Person who inherits property when somebody dies.

Some people—far too many—just say, "It will all work out." That's a comforting thought.

Unfortunately, far too often they're wrong. And they pay, financially and emotionally, for believing and trusting in fate. And their loved ones pay as well.

Many people believe the members of their family are capable of handling just about anything. They trust that their loved ones will be able to divide up estate assets fairly and with little difficulty. They think the family bond is so solid that the many details of distributing property, securities, cash, other assets, and personal items will just happen in an orderly fashion without any planning.

The reality is that all too often it doesn't work out that way. Depending on the legal complexity of the situation and the value of the assets, an estate can be held up in probate for years. That means that the courts have to sort everything out—and maybe make some decisions. This situation can strain even the most secure family relationships.

> ***Probate***—Court and legal proceedings that settle all the legal and financial matters for somebody who dies owning property.

The simple fact is that many families have suffered because somebody they loved failed to consider what might happen and neglected to prepare for the future. Old age and death cause enough suffering. Why cause further sorrow and increase the emotional and financial burdens?

With effective and thoughtful planning, you can minimize the burden on your loved ones by protecting and directing the distribution of their assets. You can decide how you want to take care of your family and your possessions with minimal or no involvement of the probate court. You can reduce or eliminate estate and income taxes, avoid many administration requirements, and facilitate the difficult process of settling your estate. If you plan wisely, you can avoid the many problems that too often leave family members feuding or confused, perhaps even deprived of what would make their lives easier.

Through estate planning, you can take care of the people you love and the things you own. It's your family. It's your things. The decision is up to you. With this book to guide you, you can do whatever you think best to prepare for the future when you will no longer be able to take care of what matters most to you.

Your Income Taxes and the Taxpayer Relief Act of 1997

Very few people enjoy reading about taxes. But it's a logical place to begin a book about estate planning. The better you understand the effect of tax laws, the better you can plan ways to reduce the taxes that threaten your estate.

Congress passed the Taxpayer Relief Act of 1997 to improve the tax situation for all of us. But that law will not provide you and your loved ones with much relief unless you understand how it affects how you take care of your estate.

You will learn the essentials about the effects of this law in this chapter and the next. We will focus first on issues involving income taxes, then on estate taxes.

We will cover nine areas in this chapter:

- Long-term capital gains
- Gain from the sale of a personal residence
- Child credit
- Education
- Individual Retirement Arrangements
- Health insurance and long-term care insurance
- Home office
- Retirement plans
- Alternative minimum tax

And we guarantee that you will not have to be a tax accountant to understand and to use what you learn in this chapter.

■ Long-Term Capital Gains

The Taxpayer Relief Act of 1997 reduced the tax rate on long-term capital gains. Previously, long-term capital gains were generally taxed at a maximum rate of 28%. The new tax law lowered this rate to 20% for many taxpayers, and to 10% for taxpayers in the 15% bracket (generally those with incomes under $41,000).

The Taxpayer Relief Act of 1997 also has shortened the holding period that qualifies capital gains as long-term and makes them eligible for lower tax rates. The holding period for long-term capital gains on sales after May 6, 1997 has been reduced from 18 months to 12 months. A special lower rate of 18% (8% for taxpayers in the 15% bracket) will apply to transactions after December 31, 2000, for assets held for more than five years.

There are at least two significant exceptions to the new reduced rate on long-term gains:

- Collectibles remain subject to the prior 28% rate. These include such items as art, antiques, and gold coins.
- Any gain due to depreciation taken on real estate will be

taxed at a rate of 25%. If the real estate is sold for more than its original cost, that portion of the gain will qualify for the new reduced rates.

There's another important point to note here. The same rules and rates that apply to capital gains under the Taxpayer Relief Act of 1997 apply for purposes of trusts and estates, and in determining income tax under the alternative minimum tax (AMT). Applying the same reduced rates when calculating the AMT on long-term capital gains should ensure that taxpayers reduce the effective tax rate on these gains.

> *Alternative Minimum Tax (AMT)*—A tax that you may pay instead of income tax if you have tax preference items or certain deductions allowed in determining regular taxable income.

■ GAIN FROM THE SALE OF A PERSONAL RESIDENCE

The tax laws have long provided for favorable tax treatment on the sale of a home. People could defer taxes on the sale if they bought another home within 24 months before or after the sale and paid at least as much for the new home as the net selling price of their old home. There was also a one-time elective exclusion for up to $125,000 of the gain from any sale of a home for those over age 55.

The Taxpayer Relief Act of 1997 replaces both these provisions with an increased exclusion available to all taxpayers.

The new rules apply to homes sold after May 6, 1997. They provide an exclusion on the gain from each home sold—up to $500,000 for a married couple and up to $250,000 for a single taxpayer. To qualify for this exclusion, the home must have been the taxpayers' primary residence for at least two of the last five years. Taxpayers can use the exclusion generally only once every two years.

The Internal Revenue Service Restructuring and Reform Act of 1998 clarifies the rules for this exclusion. Under certain circumstances, the two-year requirement need not apply. If a person who would otherwise qualify for the exclusion does not meet the two-year requirement because of certain conditions (e.g., health, change in location of employment, or unforeseen circumstances), then he or she can get an exclusion based on the fraction of the two-year period that he or she met.

Let's cut through that legalese with an example. Andrea and Bill own a house that they use as their principal residence. But just one year after they bought the house, Andrea gets a promotion that means a transfer to another state. They sell their house and make a profit of $300,000. When they file their joint tax return, they qualify for an exclusion even though they were not in the home for the two-year minimum, because of the employment change. They may exclude $250,000 (one-half the $500,000 maximum exclusion) because they were in the home for one-half of the required two years. Before the new law, it wasn't clear whether the amount excludable was a fraction of the gain on the sale or a fraction of the exclusion amount.

The new rules should eliminate any tax on the sale of a home for most families. However, new law has eliminated the old deferral provisions. This change means that taxpayers who sell a home for a gain of over $500,000 (married couple) or $250,000 (single) could incur a tax liability that would not have arisen under the old tax law.

■ CHILD CREDIT

The Taxpayer Relief Act of 1997 allows for tax credits for children *claimed as dependents* if they are under age 17 at the end of the taxable year. The tax credit is now $500 per child. (The old law did not provide tax credits based solely on the number of dependent children.)

This tax credit will be phased out for married taxpayers with an adjusted gross income (AGI) over $110,000 and for single or head of household taxpayers with an AGI over $75,000. The phaseout rate is $50 for each $1,000 of AGI over the appropriate threshold. In other words, you will not receive any credit if your AGI is above $120,000 (married) or $85,000 (single/head of household).

> ***Adjusted Gross Income***—Your gross income reduced by certain adjustments.

■ EDUCATION

If post-secondary education is part of your present or future, the Taxpayer Relief Act of 1997 can provide a little relief for you in four ways.

Educational Tuition Credit

The new tax law provides a tax credit for a portion of post-secondary education expenses, whether the student attends a college, a university, or certain vocational schools. The credit is based on tuition and related expenses. The credit is a maximum of $1,500 per year for the first two years of qualifying education, and a maximum of $1,000 per year thereafter.

In keeping with other areas of the new law, this credit is phased out for married couples with AGI between $80,000 to $90,000 and for single taxpayers with AGI between $40,000 to $50,000.

Education IRAs

The Taxpayer Relief Act of 1997 established a new concept called an *education IRA*. This allows parents to make a contribution of $500 per child under age 18 per year into this new type of IRA. The contribution is not tax-deductible.

> ***Individual Retirement Arrangement (IRA)***—A financial arrangement that allows you to contribute to an interest-earning account for a specific purpose, originally retirement but now education as well (popularly known as Individual Retirement *Account*).

As you might expect, not everybody can take advantage of the education

IRA. There are income limits for this $500 contribution. Only if your adjusted gross income (AGI) is $150,000 or less (married couples filing jointly) or $95,000 (single taxpayers) can you contribute the full amount. Between $150,000 and $160,000 (married couples filing jointly) or between $95,000 and $110,000 (single taxpayers), this contribution limit is gradually reduced. People with an AGI above those limits can't take advantage of this provision.

Any earnings on an education IRA are tax-free when withdrawn for qualifying educational expenses. If a child does not attend college, the funds must be withdrawn from the account no later than the year in which the child turns 30.

However, there are provisions that allow funds to be rolled over, tax-free, from one education IRA to another education IRA in the family. Whatever part of the IRA that is not rolled over or used for qualifying educational expenses will be subject to the early withdrawal penalty unless one of the general exceptions applies.

The list of exceptions to the 10% penalty tax for early withdrawal from IRAs includes:

- If you withdraw after age 59
- If you suffer a disability or you die
- If you make withdrawals as part of a series of substantial equal periodic payments made for life or life expectancy
- If you use the money for a first-home purchase ($10,000 maximum)
- If you use the money for higher education expenses

IRA Withdrawals for Tuition

Education IRAs are not the only way that the Taxpayer Relief Act of 1997 makes higher education more affordable. You can benefit from the new tax rules even if you don't have an education IRA—although the benefits are not quite as attractive.

The new rules allow you to withdraw money from traditional IRAs without penalty if you use it for qualifying educational expenses. The IRS will consider these withdrawals taxable income, but at least you won't be subject to the 10% penalty.

Interest on Student Loans

The new rules allow a limited deduction for interest paid on educational loans for a taxpayer and/or his or her spouse and/or dependents—even if you don't itemize. This deduction is phased in over four years, according to the following schedule:

1999	$1,500
2000	$2,000
2001	$2,500

Once again, this advantage is phased out according to AGI. This deduction is phased out between $60,000 and $75,000 for married couples and between $40,000 and $55,000 for single taxpayers.

Also note that the law states that only a taxpayer who is required to make the interest payments under the terms of the loan is allowed to deduct those payments under this provision.

INDIVIDUAL RETIREMENT ARRANGEMENTS (IRAS)

Under the old law, individuals who were active participants in an employer-sponsored retirement plan generally could not get a tax deduction for any contributions to an Individual Retirement Arrangement (IRA) if their income exceeded $35,000 (single taxpayers) or $50,000 (married couples).

Good news! The Taxpayer Relief Act of 1997 recognizes the economic realities of our times. The new law is gradually raising these income levels, to $50,000 for single taxpayers and $80,000 for married taxpayers. There's a phaseout range here as well.

On the bottom of this page is the scenario, year by year.

The rules for eligibility have changed, too. Under the new rules, a person will not be considered to be an active participant in a qualified plan simply because his or her spouse is an active participant in such a plan. That means that anybody without qualified plan coverage can take a tax deduction on contributions to an IRA.

ROTH IRAS

The Taxpayer Relief Act of 1997 also created a new form of IRA—the Roth. This new IRA is different in that it offers a terrific feature that was previously unavailable in qualified retirement plans: totally tax-free accumulation.

> ***Roth IRA***—Individual Retirement Arrangement that differs from the traditional IRA in that contributions are not tax-deductible but withdrawals are tax-free.

Investors can establish and build a Roth IRA in two ways:

- Contributions
- Conversions—transfers from traditional IRAs

Year	single taxpayer	married filing jointly
1999	$31,000-$41,000	$51,000-$61,000
2000	$32,000-$42,000	$52,000-$62,000
2001	$33,000-$43,000	$53,000-$63,000
2002	$34,000-$44,000	$54,000-$64,000
2003	$40,000-$50,000	$60,000-$70,000
2004	$45,000-$50,000	$65,000-$75,000
2005	$50,000-$60,000	$70,000-$80,000
2006	$50,000-$60,000	$75,000-$85,000
2007	$50,000-$60,000	$80,000-$100,000

Whichever method you choose to fund your Roth IRA, you cannot take a tax deduction. That money is "after-tax dollars," as we'll explain.

Contributions

The Roth IRA allows annual nondeductible contributions of up to $2,000 of earned income for singles and $4,000 for married couples who file jointly ($2,000 per spouse). The maximum contribution is subject to annual Adjusted Gross Income (AGI) ceilings—$95,000 for single taxpayers and $150,000 for couples filing a joint return. The amount allowable is gradually reduced above those ceilings, to down to zero for AGIs of $110,000 or higher (single) or $160,000 or higher (married filing jointly).

Some bad news: the annual $2,000 contribution limit for a Roth IRA is reduced by contributions to any traditional (non-Roth) IRA for a given year. But there's good news as well: any conversions from a traditional IRA to a Roth IRA (discussed below) are not considered contributions, so you should not include them in calculating the AGI or as IRA contributions in determining Roth eligibility.

Conversions

You can convert funds from a traditional IRA into a Roth IRA if your AGI is $100,000 or less. Surprise! This ceiling is the same whether you're single or married filing jointly. (If you're married filing separately, however, you cannot convert.)

All conversions to Roth IRAs are treated as distributions. That means that the money is subject to ordinary income tax rates, so proceed with caution: consider the time horizon for the Roth IRA as well as the tax consequences. All taxes that are due must be accountable in the year of the conversion.

A substantial portion, if not all, of the conversion is likely to be subject to taxation at ordinary income rates, depending on the proportion of nondeductible contributions, deductible contributions, and accumulated earnings in the conversion amount. Only nondeductible contributions are not subject to taxation.

What all that verbiage means in simple terms is that if you have not yet paid taxes on the money that you're converting, you must do so now. Uncle Sam either got a cut back when you put the money into the IRA or will get a cut now when you convert it to a Roth.

Furthermore, the aggregate balance of all IRAs owned must be factored to determine taxable income resulting from the conversion. For example, if you have one deductible IRA and one nondeductible IRA, you must consider the proportionate percentages of both IRAs (in terms of accumulated earnings and deductible and nondeductible contributions) for tax purposes—even if you transfer funds from the nondeductible IRA only.

So far we've discussed only conversions from other IRAs into Roth IRAs. But it's also possible to cancel a Roth conversion and revert to a traditional IRA.

Why would you do that? You might cancel and revert if your AGI unexpectedly rose above $100,000 (which would preclude a conversion) or you suffered a severe decline in net asset value after the conversion (to avoid declaring higher taxable amounts). However, the law allows you only one conversion reversal for any tax year, so choose wisely.

Withdrawals

Because your contributions to a Roth IRA are nondeductible, you can withdraw your *contributions* without paying any tax or penalty. You can do so at any time, without restriction.

And, if you've held the Roth IRA at least five years, you can withdraw *accumulated earnings* without paying taxes if you meet one of the following qualified exemptions:

- You reach the minimum age of 59
- You use the money for a first-time home purchase (maximum of $10,000)
- You become disabled
- You die

As for withdrawing amounts attributable to *conversions,* that situation has been clarified by the Tax Technical Corrections Act of 1998. The clarifications may seem complicated, but they were necessary.

A big loophole in the Taxpayer Relief Act of 1997 allowed people to convert traditional IRAs to a Roth IRA, declare the taxable income from a 1998 conversion over four years, and then immediately withdraw those conversion amounts without any additional tax ramifications. Ooops!

That loophole no longer exists, because the technical corrections impose a waiting period of five tax years, beginning with the year of first conversion. (We'll discuss this a little later, in the section on Taxes and Penalties in this chapter.)

The technical corrections also impose ordering or distribution rules, to eliminate confusion about the four types of sources for the money in a Roth IRA. After all, the money in your Roth could be there through contributions, through conversion from deductible IRAs, through conversion from nondeductible IRAs, or from interest. What that means is that, when you withdraw money, it's considered to come out in the following order:

1. Contributions
2. Any conversion amounts that were subject to taxation, on a first-in first-out basis
3. Any conversion amounts that were not subject to taxation upon conversion
4. Accumulated earnings

Those ordering rules may seem confusing at first, but they simplify withdrawals. They also eliminate the need for separate Roth IRA accounts for contributions and conversions, which would further complicate your life.

> ***Ordering rules***—Procedure for determining the status of withdrawals from Roth IRAs, as established by the Tax Technical Corrections Act of 1998.

Finally, unlike other types of IRAs, the Roth IRA has no mandatory withdrawal age or minimum distribution requirements. If you wish, you can hold your Roth IRA indefinitely, without ever taking any money out. Then, when you die, your heirs would receive the Roth IRA proceeds, which would be entirely free from federal income taxes—unlike other IRAs.

Taxes and Penalties

As we've mentioned, any withdrawals of *contributions* from a Roth IRA are tax-free and penalty-free at any time. That's simple enough—for contributions.

Withdrawals from *conversion* amounts are also tax-free and penalty-free—if you've held the conversion amounts for at least five years. But if you withdraw from conversion amounts within five tax years of your first conversion and are under age 59, then a 10% early withdrawal tax penalty would apply to all withdrawn conversion amounts for that year.

After you've withdrawn all your contributions and all your conversion amounts, the subsequent withdrawals would be from accumulated earnings. (Remember those ordering rules!) If you have not met at least one of the qualified exemptions discussed for withdrawals, then all early withdrawals of accumulated earnings are taxed at ordinary income rates plus a 10% early withdrawal tax penalty.

The 10% tax penalty on early withdrawals from conversions and accumulated earnings is waived for the following exceptions:

- Death
- Disability
- Equal periodic payment withdrawals over owner's life expectancy
- Medical expenses greater than 7.5% of AGI
- Health insurance premiums for an unemployed person
- Qualified higher-education expenses
- First-time home purchase

Strategies

The Roth IRA is not intended to replace a Keogh or 401(k) plan, especially if your employer matches a portion of your 401(k) contributions. Ideally, after maximizing these Keogh or 401(k) plans, the Roth IRA should be your next investment priority, since earnings grow tax-free and withdrawals are tax-free. That's a terrific combination—if you can meet the minimum holding requirement of five years and meet one of the qualified withdrawal requirements.

Many investors may also face a decision between the Roth IRA and either a nondeductible IRA or a deductible IRA. So how do you decide?

The Roth IRA is the clear choice over the *nondeductible* IRA; both are very similar, except that earnings withdrawn from the Roth IRA are tax-free, while earnings withdrawn from a nondeductible IRA are taxable at ordinary income rates.

The choice between the Roth IRA and a *deductible* IRA is more complicated. You need to compare the front-end tax savings and the taxes on withdrawals from the deductible IRA, on the one hand, and the up-front taxes and the tax-free accumulations from the Roth, on the other hand. You should consider your present and future tax brackets. As a general rule, if your tax rate will be higher at withdrawal, choose the Roth; if it will be lower, choose the deductible IRA. If you believe that your tax rate will be unchanged, some analysts give the edge to the Roth, while others call it a dead heat. However, investors with a long-term time horizon are likely to prefer the Roth over the deductible IRA, because the earnings can be considerable with time, so the tax advantage is greater.

Another decision is whether to convert a traditional IRA to a Roth IRA. The most important factors here are tax consequences and time horizon. The key is to compare the taxes you would pay now in making the conversion and the taxes you would save in the future on accumulated earnings from the Roth IRA. Generally, if you're close to retiring, you probably should not convert to a Roth IRA. However, if you have a long-term time horizon and if you can afford to pay the taxes on your regular IRA, then a conversion to a Roth IRA would be beneficial.

In summary, whether your goal is to supplement your retirement income, to add to your estate, or to make a first-time home purchase, the Roth IRA offers a benefit of tax-free accumulation that was previously unavailable in qualified plans. As long as you meet the minimum holding and withdrawal requirements, this new type of IRA is a vehicle that you can use to achieve your goal. (We'll discuss IRAs further in Chapter 8, Planning for Your Retirement.)

■ NET OPERATING LOSS CARRYOVERS

The old tax law allowed taxpayers to carry net operating losses (NOLs) back three years and forward 15 years to offset any taxable income in those years. The Taxpayer Relief Act of 1997 revises these periods to allow taxpayers to carry NOLs back only two years but forward 20 years. Farmers get a little break here: a farming loss may be carried back for five years.

These new periods will not apply to NOLs arising from casualty losses or NOLs attributable to losses incurred by small businesses or taxpayers engaged in a farming business in locations declared as presidential disaster areas.

■ SELF-EMPLOYED HEALTH INSURANCE AND LONG-TERM CARE INSURANCE DEDUCTION

People who are self-employed are currently able to deduct 60% for tax years 1999, 2000, and 2001 of the health insurance premiums paid for themselves, their spouses, and dependents. This percentage is scheduled to increase to 70% for 2002 and 100% for 2003.

■ OFFICE IN HOME

In 1993, a U.S. Supreme Court case restricted the availability of deductions for the business use of a home. This decision required that the home office be the place in which the *primary* business activity takes place. This eliminated the deduction for many self-employed individuals who worked out of their homes but also provided services or met with their customers elsewhere.

The new rules eliminate the primary business activity test and allow home office expenses to be deducted if the taxpayer has no other fixed business location.

■ RETIREMENT PLAN CHANGES

The Taxpayer Relief Act of 1997 made a number of changes in the area of qualified plans. One of the most important was that it repealed the 15% excise tax on excess distributions and accumulations. The tax on distributions had previously been suspended for distributions in 1997, 1998, or 1999. The new law permanently repeals the excise tax on both. As a result, you may need to re-examine estate and financial plans.

■ ALTERNATIVE MINIMUM TAX

In case you're thinking about skipping this section, please read this paragraph at least. Many people who prepare their own income tax returns and some tax return preparers have ignored the AMT because they aren't aware of it, don't understand it, or believe it doesn't apply. However, the tax applies more and more often, even to many middle-class taxpayers. So we encourage you to read on.

First, a little history, by way of explanation. The tax laws give preferential treatment to certain kinds of income and allow special deductions and credits for some kinds of expenses. The Alternative Minimum Tax (AMT) was created so taxpayers with substantial income would pay some tax. Before the AMT, many taxpayers had substantial income but avoided paying income taxes by using tax deductions, incentive tax credits, and tax shelter investments. The purpose of the AMT is to ensure that all people who benefit from these tax advantages will pay at least some taxes.

The AMT is a separate tax computation that in effect eliminates many deductions and credits, thus increasing the tax liability for an individual who would otherwise pay little or no tax.

You may have to pay the AMT if your taxable income for regular tax purposes plus any of the adjustments and preference items that apply to you is more than the exemption amount. The exemption amounts are:

- $45,000 if you are married filing jointly or you are a qualifying widow or widower
- $33,750 if you are single or head of household
- $22,500 if you are married filing separately or for an estate or a trust

Among the major deductions disallowed in computing the AMT are itemized deductions for property taxes, state personal income taxes, and certain miscellaneous itemized deductions. Interest expense from home equity lines of credit may also be disallowed.

Many changes have been made to the AMT over the years. Most significantly, graduated tax rates were added to the tax computation, replacing the original flat tax.

The income tax is computed using the regular tax tables and then alternative minimum tax is computed; the higher amount is usually paid. Before the capital gains exclusion was repealed, it was one of the most common AMT preferences added back to regular income. The Taxpayer Relief Act of 1997 restored this tax preference.

Old tax law called for an AMT adjustment for differences between AMT depreciation and regular tax depreciation. The Taxpayer Relief Act of 1997 eliminates depreciation differences in most cases for property that is placed into service after 1998.

The old law did not allow farmers to defer the recognition of income for AMT by using the installment method on the installment sale of personal property. The new tax law allows cash-method farmers to use the installment method of accounting for AMT, retroactive to taxable years beginning after December 31, 1987.

The new law also contains an exemption from the AMT for small businesses (other than personal service corporations) with less than $5,000,000 of gross receipts.

As we mentioned earlier, many people have ignored the AMT. They could pay a price for ignoring it. However, the AMT tax applies to more and more people every year. About 605,000 taxpayers paid the AMT in 1997. According to the congressional Joint Committee on Taxation, that number could grow to 6.2 million by 2005, assuming an inflation rate of only 3% percent a year, and 8.4 million by 2007. Are you among the millions of taxpayers who should be paying serious attention to the AMT?

Inflation is eroding tax exemptions and brackets. But, unlike the standard tax system, the AMT is not indexed for inflation. Factor in the new nonrefundable child and tuition credits—two preference items not allowed under the AMT—and more people than ever risk what has been labeled a "tax trap" or a "shadow tax."

It's important to consider the ramifications of the AMT when preparing income tax planning computations. People who plan their tax situation in advance can avoid wasting deductions disallowed under the AMT. They can also prepare in advance for the cash required to pay the tax, be sure they meet estimated tax payment requirements, and plan to use minimum tax credits—all components of a thoughtfully crafted income tax strategy.

3 Your Estate Taxes and the Taxpayer Relief Act of 1997

Uncle Sam doesn't really care whether you're dead or alive—at least in terms of when you give away your property. Your gifts (what you give away while living) or bequests (what you give away when you die) are lumped together as subject to estate and gift taxes.

The estate and gift tax is a transfer tax assessed on property that changes possession. It's called a *unified* tax because the same tax rates, deductions, and rules apply to both gifts and estate.

> ***Transfer tax***—A tax imposed when ownership of property passes from one person to another.

Uncle Sam has a heart when it comes to generosity. The tax laws establish a unified credit exemption. What this means is that you can give away a certain amount of assets, during your lifetime or upon your death, without incurring a federal estate or gift tax. That concept seems simple enough, but it results in some complicated calculations.

> ***Unified credit exemption***—The amount of property that an individual can give away through gifts or an estate.

A LITTLE HISTORY

To understand the impact of the Taxpayer Relief Act of 1997, let's get some recent historical perspective of the gift and estate tax laws in the United States.

In 1981, the federal estate tax laws provided an exemption of $175,625. In other words, if an adjusted gross estate was less than that amount, it paid no estate tax. In 1982 the law was changed. Under the revised law, the exemption began to rise until 1987, when it reached $600,000. That was the magic figure for 10 years: if the adjusted gross estate was less than $600,000, no federal estate taxes were imposed.

The Taxpayer Relief Act of 1997 provides for the estate tax exemption to again increase incrementally, beginning in 1998 with a $625,000 unified credit exemption and ending in 2006 at $1,000,000. If your generosity (gifts and estate) exceeds that amount, it's subject to marginal tax rates, starting at 37% and reaching 60%, then dropping to 55%. (See Figure 3a, page 18.)

> ***Marginal tax***—The tax imposed on an estate that is valued in excess of the unified credit exemption, when the value of lifetime gifts has been included.

In addition, Uncle Sam recognizes that families that own businesses should not be treated the same as other families. The Taxpayer Relief Act of 1997 provides special estate tax relief

Estate Tax Exemptions Under The Tax Relief Act Of 1997

Year	Exemption Amount(a)	Unified Credit(b)
1999	$650,000	$211,300
2000	$675,000	$220,550
2001	$675,000	$220,550
2002	$700,000	$229,800
2003	$700,000	$229,800
2004	$850,000	$287,300
2005	$950,000	$326,300
2006	$1,000,000	$345,800

FIGURE 3A

for family-owned businesses. If a business meets certain criteria, it will be eligible for an additional exemption. There are restrictions on this special exemption, which we'll examine later in this chapter.

■ GIFT TAXES

Under the old law, an individual could not give anyone any gifts that exceeded $10,000 per person per year without creating a gift tax liability for the generous individual. But that limit did not take into account a very important economic reality—inflation.

> *Gift tax*—A tax imposed on the transfer of property while alive, to be paid by the person giving the gift, if the value of the gift(s) is greater than the annual allowable limit.

The Taxpayer Relief Act of 1997 provides for inflation. The new law indexes the maximum amount allowable, starting in 1999. The method for indexing is based on the Consumer Price Index (CPI), which is a federal measurement of the value of a dollar, in terms of what we can buy with our money.

> *Consumer Price Index (CPI)*—A federal measurement of inflation and deflation based on changes in the relative costs of goods and services for a typical consumer.

That's good news, in theory. However, because of how the indexing is calculated—in increments of $1,000—that max may remain at $10,000 for a while. In fact, given the current low rate of inflation, it may be at least a few years before we see any substantial increase.

If you're married, you and your spouse can combine your maximum amounts. You can do this even if the property belongs to just one of the spouses—even if you're not living in one of the community property states. That's nice of Uncle Sam—or maybe it just makes sense, since spouses can give each other gifts without incurring any gift taxes.

What's a gift? Generally when people talk about "gifts," it seems fairly straightforward. A gift is something of some value what you give to somebody. But when the IRS gets involved, we need a definition and, of course, some exceptions.

So, a gift is any transaction in which property or property interests are voluntarily transferred to another without adequate consideration. This definition does not include future interests, gifts that the recipient can use only in the future.

> *Gift*—Any voluntary transfer of property or property interests to another without adequate consideration.

Here are a few exceptions. The federal gift tax does not apply to:

- Gifts to spouse
- Gifts to tax-exempt organizations, such as charities and religious entities
- Gifts to schools
- Gifts to governmental agencies
- Loans to family members at interest rates below the market rate
- College tuition paid directly to the institution (not the student!)
- Medical expenses paid directly to the institution (not the patient!)

> **Note:** If you make over $10,000 in gifts to a qualified charitable organization, you must file IRS Form 709, the Federal Gift Tax Return. You won't pay a gift tax, but the IRS likes to keep track of big gifts.

What happens if you exceed the exemption amount for gifts to one person in a single year? Then you must file IRS Form 709. Of course, you don't need to put yourself in that situation, if you do the proper financial planning.

■ ESTATE TAXES

How does the estate tax work? First, an estate is inventoried to determine its total value. There are certain deductions that can be subtracted from the estate, including funeral expenses, administration and attorney's fees, income taxes to be paid, and debts and mortgages.

> *Estate tax*—A tax imposed on the estate when it transfers to heirs (also known as inheritance tax or death tax).

The adjusted value of the estate is compiled. That amount is then referenced on the unified federal estate and gift tax table. (See Figure 3b.) From the estate tax, the estate is allowed to deduct the unified credit to arrive at the taxes that are due. The unified

Unified Federal Gift And Estate Tax Table

Dollar Value Of Taxable Transfer (a)	Federal Unified Tax Before Credits (b)	Percent Of Excess (c)
$0	$0	18%
$10,000	$1,800	20%
$20,000	$3,800	22%
$40,000	$8,200	24%
$60,000	$13,000	26%
$80,000	$18,200	28%
$100,000	$23,800	30%
$150,000	$38,800	32%
$200,000	$54,800	32%
$250,000	$70,800	34%
$300,000	$87,800	34%
$400,000	$121,800	34%
$500,000	$155,800	37%
$600,000	$192,800	37%
$700,000	$229,800	37%
$750,000	$248,300	39%
$800,000	$267,800	39%
$900,000	$306,800	39%
$1,000,000	$345,800	41%
$1,100,000	$386,800	41%
$1,250,000	$448,300	43%
$1,500,000	$555,800	45%
$1,600,000	$600,800	45%
$2,000,000	$780,800	49%
$2,100,000	$829,800	49%
$2,500,000	$1,025,800	53%
$2,600,000	$1,078,800	53%
$3,000,000	$1,290,800	55%
$10,000,000	$5,140,800	60%
$21,225,000	$11,875,800	55%

Key:
(a) Base value of taxable estate.
(b) Base tax on estate.
(c) Percent tax on excess.
* Rate drops to 55% over $21,225,000

FIGURE 3B

credit amount is equal to the estate taxes on an equivalent estate exemption.

The terminology makes this calculation seem more complicated than it actually is. For example, in 1999 the unified credit is $211,300, which is the amount of tax due on a $650,000 estate. The significance of this method of calculation is that the estate does not deduct the credit exemption first, but rather after the tax level is determined. Thus, the estate is taxed at the highest possible level before the exemption is used.

■ THE BOTTOM LINE

The increase in unified credits and corresponding equivalent exemptions enacted in the Taxpayer Relief Act of 1997 looks good—at first glance. A closer examination reveals that the $600,000 exemption that was available in 1987, then indexed at a 3% annual rate, would have been $806,350 by year 1997. In year 2006 it projects to $1,052,104. (See Figure 3c.) Many estates are growing at a much faster rate than inflation.

> Conclusion: The new estate tax law is not quite keeping pace with inflation. Estate planning is more important than ever.

UNLIMITED MARITAL DEDUCTION

Under the Federal Uniform Estate and Gift Tax rules, there are provisions that, if used properly, allow estates to reduce the impact of estate taxes. One of these rules is the unlimited marital deduction. Simply put, a person can leave an estate of any size to his or her surviving spouse without paying any estate taxes.

> AS SIMPLE AS 1, 2, 3...
> 1. Many estates are growing at a much faster rate than inflation.
> 2. The new estate tax law is not quite keeping pace with inflation.
> 3. Estate planning is more important than ever.

> *Unlimited marital deduction*—A legal provision that allows a person to give gifts of any size or pass an estate of any size to his or her spouse, without any gift or estate taxes or using any part of the unified credit.

If the estates of both spouses combined are over $650,000, you should do some planning so that each of you can take advantage of your own $650,000 exemption. If you don't use your exemption, it disappears when you die: your surviving spouse can't use it.

(Why do we use an exemption of $650,000 here, if this exemption is scheduled to rise almost every year until 2006? We'll answer that question with another: When are you going to die? Death is just a fact of life. We intend to live for years, but we must plan as if we could die at any moment. That's why we use the 1999 exemption in our explanation.)

If, however, the combined estates were considerably higher, over $1,300,000, then you'd have to pay some taxes if you were to die at this

Indexing Of The Unified Credit From 1987 to 2006

Year	Projected Increase Annually (a)	Projected Increase Exemption (b)	Existing And Future Exemption (c)	Net Difference Projected (d)
1987	$0	$600,000	$600,000	$0
1988	$18,000	$618,000	$600,000	($18,000)
1989	$18,540	$636,540	$600,000	($36,540)
1990	$19,096	$655,636	$600,000	($55,636)
1991	$19,669	$675,305	$600,000	($75,305)
1992	$20,259	$695,564	$600,000	($95,564)
1993	$20,867	$716,431	$600,000	($116,431)
1994	$21,493	$737,924	$600,000	($137,924)
1995	$22,138	$760,062	$600,000	($160,062)
1996	$22,802	$782,864	$600,000	($182,864)
1997	$23,486	$806,350	$600,000	($206,350)
1998	$24,190	$830,540	$625,000	($205,540)
1999	$24,916	$855,457	$650,000	($205,457)
2000	$25,664	$881,120	$675,000	($206,120)
2001	$26,434	$907,554	$675,000	($232,554)
2002	$27,227	$934,780	$700,000	($234,780)
2003	$28,043	$962,824	$700,000	($262,824)
2004	$28,885	$991,709	$850,000	($141,709)
2005	$29,751	$1,021,460	$950,000	($71,460)
2006	$30,644	$1,052,104	$1,000,000	($52,104)

Key:

(a) Hypothetical projected annual increase of estate tax exemption indexed from 1987 at 3 %.

(b) Hypothetical projected estate tax exemption indexed from 1987 at 3 %.

(c) Actual estate tax exemption through year 2006.

(d) Hypothetical projected shortfall of actual exemption compared to indexed 3 % exemption since 1987.

FIGURE 3C

moment. If that seems unlikely, you'll want to continue reading. We've got some suggestions for managing that estate so the tax burden will be less.

■ HOW TO REDUCE ESTATE TAXES

Using the unlimited marital deduction will certainly reduce taxes when the first spouse dies. However, the estate that passes to the surviving spouse increases his or her estate. That growth is ultimately taxed, when the second spouse dies. So using the marital deduction can hurt your heirs. To avoid this unfortunate tax situation, it's wise to balance the value of both spouse's estates whenever possible.

Figure 3d illustrates a scenario from 1999. (Again, we're using current fig-

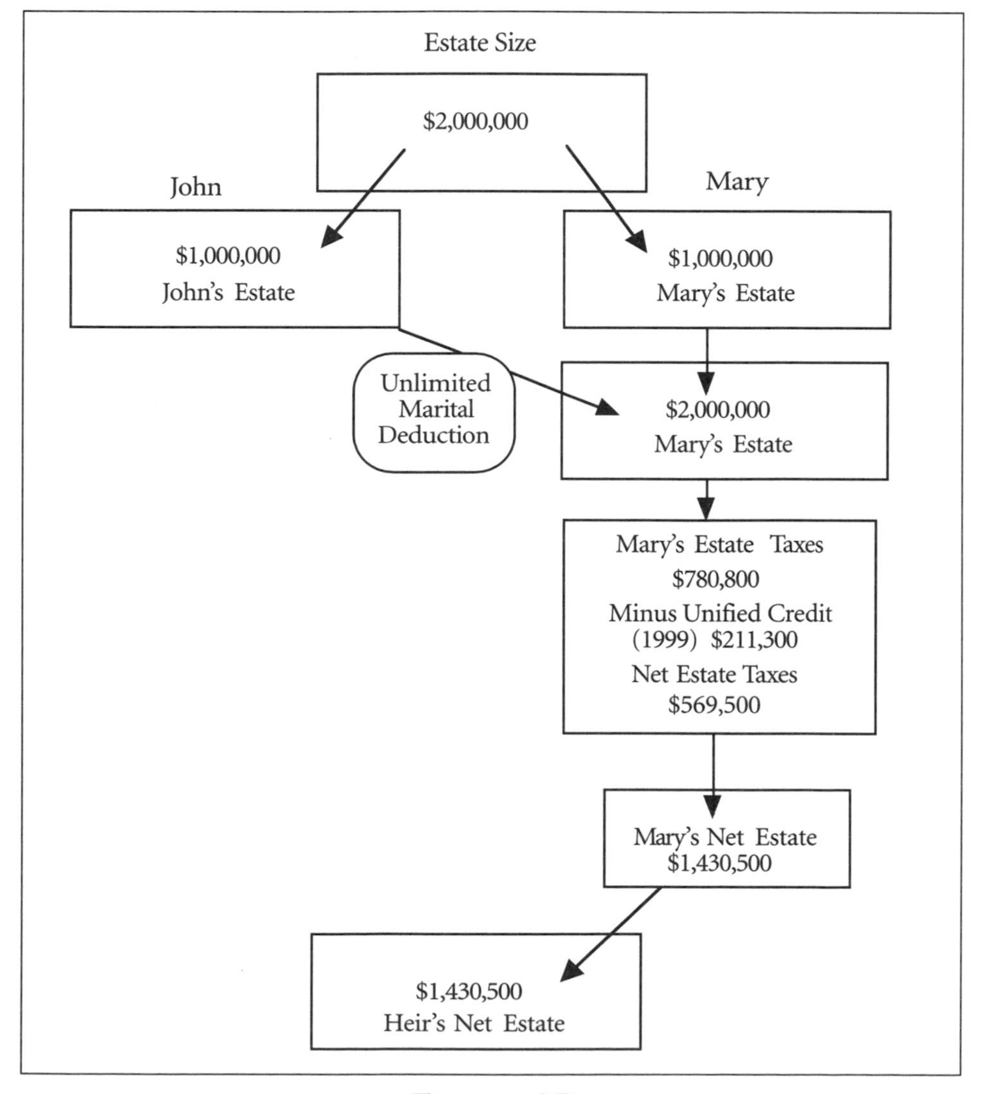

FIGURE 3D

ures for the sake of simplicity. We could show the same principles at work for 2006, with the exemption and credit that will be in effect that year.)

John and Mary have an estate valued at $2,000,000. John dies, leaving all of his estate to Mary. Because of the unlimited marital deduction, Mary receives John's $1,000,000 without any loss to estate taxes. When Mary dies, however, the entire $2,000,000 is subject to estate taxes.

The gift and federal estate tax table (Figure 3b) shows those taxes to be $780,800. With the current (1999) unified credit of $211,300 (Figure 3a, the unified credit equivalent to the $650,000 exemption), the taxes amount to $569,500. (So Uncle Sam takes a 28.475% bite out of the estate.

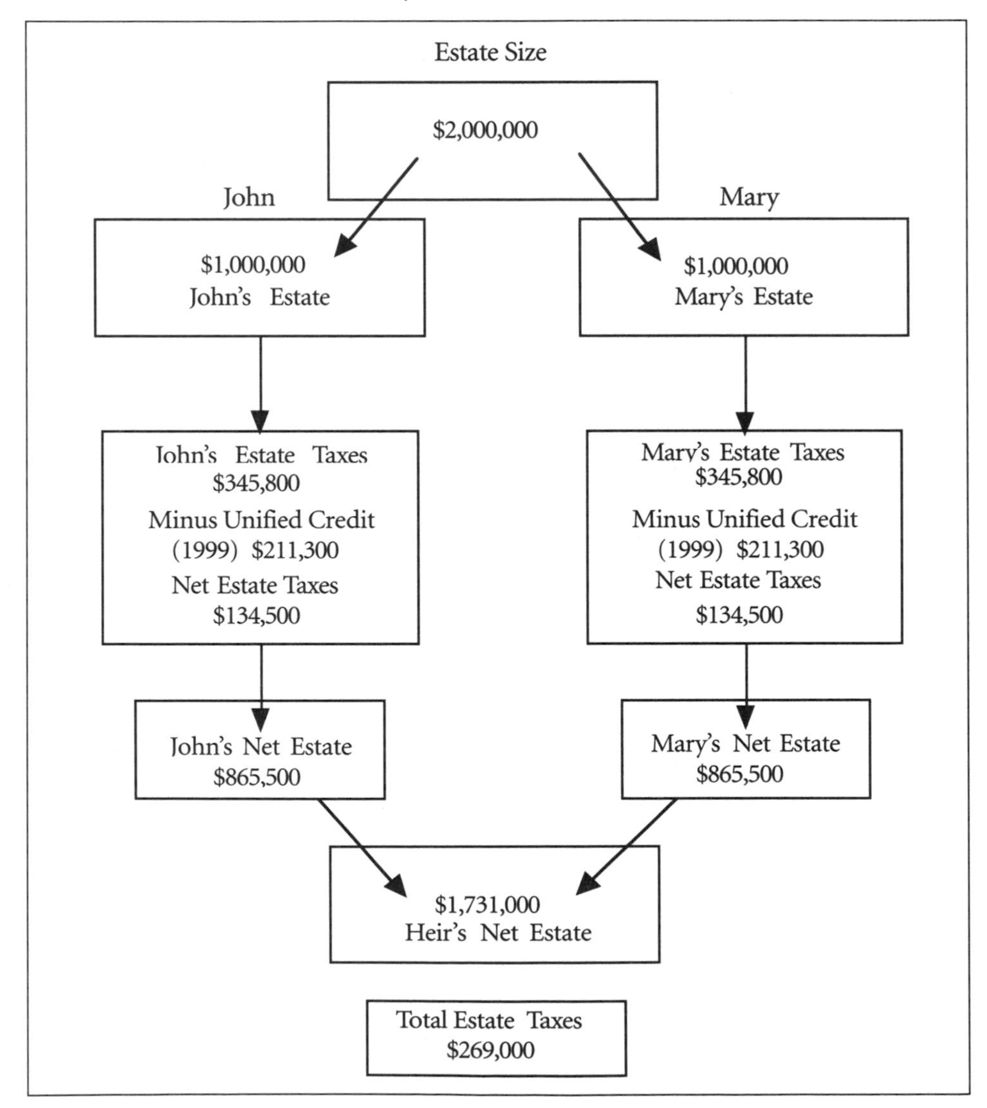

FIGURE 3E

Much of that $569,500 loss for John's and Mary's heir was unnecessary, since John's unified credit estate exemption of $650,000 went unused.

Now, let's try a little estate planning. Figure 3e shows how we can structure their estate to reduce that tax bite.

When John dies, his $1,000,000 goes to his heirs, not to Mary. The taxes on his estate are $345,800 (Figure 3b), but with his unified credit estate exemption of $211,300 (Figure 3a, the unified credit equivalent to the $650,000 exemption), the federal estate tax drops to $134,500. The estate tax liability on the combined estates of John and Mary is reduced by $269,000.

That's much better than the $569,500 lost in the scenario in Figure 3d. That simple strategy of willing $1,000,000 directly to the heir reduced the tax bite to 13.45%.

Note this very important and interesting point: the amount of estate tax saved here by distributing John's and Mary's estates separately exceeded the value of John's unified credit that went unused when his estate passed to Mary. His unified credit was $211,300, but when used properly it saved $300,500 in estate taxes.

This estate planning point is too often overlooked. This occurs because the estate tax system is a marginal tax rate system. It taxes an estate at the top brackets of the adjusted estate's value. The tax is imposed on the value of an estate in excess of the unified credit.

John and Mary used a simple strategy to keep a lot of money away from Uncle Sam for their heir. We'll discuss more advanced estate planning techniques in later chapters. We will also look at using the marital deduction in combination with other strategies.

■ THE GENERATION-SKIPPING TAX

Tax planners have often recommended trusts and other devices as ways to pass property down through several generations with no estate tax burden. The advantage was to provide income from the property to the following generation without incurring any estate transfer tax, since the heirs would not inherit any rights to the property itself. In other words, the transfer would skip a generation or more.

The Tax Reform Act of 1976 imposed a new tax and new tax return requirement on such an arrangement. This Act was repealed and replaced by legislation in the Tax Reform Act of 1986. The generation-skipping transfer tax is imposed on every generation-skipping transfer, whether in trust or through direct distributions. However, the generation-skipping transfer tax does not apply to lifetime annual exclusion gifts to individuals and to certain trusts or to certain transfers for medical or educational purposes.

> ***Generation skipping tax***—Tax imposed on trusts and other devices that would otherwise allow you to provide your heirs with income from property yet bypass estate transfer tax.

Each person has a $1,000,000 exemption from the generation-skipping tax. The exemption has been indexed to the consumer price index formula. Because of the way the formula works, we do not actually anticipate any increase for several years.

DISCLAIMERS

Here's another simple way to reduce or avoid estate taxes. And it's not an idea that would occur to most people.

We're all familiar with the term "disclaimer" as it's generally used. It's a way to not take responsibility for something—usually through a lot of fine print. In the case of estate planning, the term has a somewhat different meaning: what the person is disclaiming is property.

Let's put that difference into legal terms. A disclaimer is an irrevocable and unqualified refusal by a person to accept an interest in property. The disclaimed property will be treated as though it had never been transferred to the person making the disclaimer. This action can suit various positive purposes and provide significant benefits, financial and otherwise.

> ***Disclaimer***—Refusal to accept property that is passed on through a will.

Why would anybody want to refuse to accept taking possession of inherited property? As we said, it's not an idea that would occur to most people.

There are various situations in which it might make sense to disclaim an inheritance. Consider the following examples:

- A named beneficiary can essentially make a tax-free gift to another person by disclaiming an inheritance—if the inheritance would, under state law, go to the second person.
- A will leaves the entire estate to two children, but unequally. The child designated to receive the larger share might disclaim part of that share in order to make the split more equitable.
- A surviving spouse doesn't need the property. He or she might disclaim it in order to avoid estate taxes when his or her property passes on later to the children.
- A child who is financially comfortable inherits a share of a parent's estate. He or she could disclaim that inheritance so that it passes into a trust established in the will for his or her children, to add to the share designated specifically for them.
- A significant portion of a taxable estate is held in the husband's name and the wife's estate is less than the personal exemption amount. The wife dies first; in her will she leaves everything to the husband. The husband disclaims the assets, which then pass to the heirs, using a portion of the deceased spouse's unified credit/personal exemption.

Disclaiming the inheritance can be an effective strategy when a will is outdated. Let's take an example.

When your rich uncle drew up his will 20 years ago, you (his favorite nephew) were struggling to pay off some bills and take care of your two young children. So he willed all his $100,000 to you, with the provision that it would go to your kids if you died before your uncle. Unfortunately, your uncle dies without updating his will to take into account the current situation. Now, 20 years later, you're quite wealthy and your two kids are trying to make it through graduate school.

You know that your uncle would want his money to go to your children now, since they need it more than you do. Of course, you could accept the inheritance and then give the money to your children. But then you'd have to give them only $10,000 each per year or pay gift taxes. Either way, they lose. A disclaimer allows you to do what your uncle would want. By using a disclaimer, you can, in effect, step out of the way of the inheritance and let it go directly to your children.

A disclaimer can also be useful when there's no will at all. If the state laws dictate that the inheritance should pass to you, rather than to another relative, who would be second in line to inherit, you can respect the unwritten wishes of the deceased and disclaim the inheritance, so that it passes to the next heir in line.

So, how do you make a disclaimer?

For the purposes of federal estate, gift, and generation-skipping transfer taxes, you must meet the following requirements:

- The refusal must be in writing.
- The disclaimer must be irrevocable and unqualified.
- The written refusal must be received by the transferor, his or her legal representative, or the holder of the legal title not more than nine months after the date on which the transfer is made or the date on which that person reaches age 21, whichever comes later.
- The person making the disclaimer must not have accepted the property or any of its benefits.
- The property must pass to someone other than the person making the disclaimer.
- The property must pass without any direction from the person disclaiming the property. That means he or she cannot direct to whom the disclaimed property should go. (Before deciding to disclaim, the person should know who is next in line to receive the property, according to the terms of the will and/or state law.)

You've got to be careful about meeting each of these requirements. If you don't, you will be considered the legal recipient of the property. But that's not all: you will then be deemed to have gifted the property that you were trying to disclaim. In other words, you may achieve the outcome you desired—the beneficiary may receive the property—but achieving it through a gift transfer rather than through a proper disclaimer can mean you'll be paying a gift tax for your generosity. Also, if the recipient of your generosity is two generations below you, the generation-skipping transfer tax may also be imposed. Ouch!

We should mention that you don't have to be generous to an extreme. It's possible to make only a partial disclaimer, that is, to disclaim only part of the property that you would otherwise inherit. In this case as well, you must meet all the statutory requirements listed above.

In addition, a partial disclaimer of property will be respected only on the following two conditions:

- The portion disclaimed must be severable from the part accepted.
- The disclaimer must identify the specific assets being disclaimed.

In other words, you cannot disclaim half of the family mansion (the house cannot be severed) or half of the sports car collection (the description is too vague).

As you might guess, despite the extra complications, this means of accepting some property while disclaiming the rest can be quite useful.

Any beneficiary considering disclaiming an inheritance should consult with an estate planner. If the property disclaimed is large enough, it could result in a generation-skipping transfer tax. Some cynics claim that no good deed goes unpunished. If you're not careful, you could prove that point.

■ CHANGES FOR FAMILY-OWNED BUSINESSES

As we mentioned earlier, when it comes to estate taxes, Uncle Sam treats a family differently if it owns a business. There's particular relief in the Taxpayer Relief Act of 1997 for family-owned businesses.

The new law created an estate tax exemption that can mean a total exemption of as much as $1.3 million for qualified family-owned businesses. This estate tax exemption can be taken only to the extent that it exceeds the personal estate exemption. In other words, when the unified credit exempts $625,000 of an estate, the business exemption covers an additional $675,000.

That's a great benefit for a family-owned business. However, it will be a little less good as the years pass. That $1,300,000 remains constant but, as we have discussed, the personal estate exemption will rise incrementally to $1,000,000 in 2006. As a result, the business benefit will decline to a $300,000 equivalent exemption by 2006. (See Figure 3f.)

So much for the math. Now it's time for some legal definitions.

Who can take advantage of that new exemption? The law defines "qualifying family-owned business" in terms of four requirements, as:

1. any interest in a trade or business (regardless of the actual form of the business)
2. with a principal place of business in the United States
3. if the ownership is held at least 50% by one family, 70% by two families, or 90% by three families, and

Estate Tax Exemptions Under The Tax Relief Act Of 1997

Year	Exemption Amount(a)	Family Business Exclusion(b)	Maximum Combined Exclusion(c)
1999	$650,000	$650,000	$1,300,000
2000	$675,000	$625,000	$1,300,000
2001	$675,000	$625,000	$1,300,000
2002	$700,000	$600,000	$1,300,000
2003	$700,000	$600,000	$1,300,000
2004	$850,000	$450,000	$1,300,000
2005	$950,000	$350,000	$1,300,000
2006	$1,000,000	$300,000	$1,300,000

Key:

(a) The amount each individual estate is allowed as an exemption.

(b) The new family business exclusion. The business will have restrictions for eligibility.

(c) The maximum combined exclusion for a family owned business cannot exceed $1,300,000.

FIGURE 3F

4. as long as the decedent's family owns at least 30% of the trade or business.

How does the law define "family"? To qualify for inclusion in the above percentages, you must be in one of the following categories: the decedent's spouse, the decedent's parents, the decedent's grandparents, the decedent's children and their spouses, the decedent's spouse's children and their spouses, and the decedent's brothers and sisters and their spouses.

The total value of the qualified family-owned business interest that is passed to qualified heirs must be more than 50% of the decedent's adjusted gross estate. This is known as the 50% test. It's more complicated than we're presenting it here, so again we advise consulting an estate planner.

Now, we've got another term to define—qualified heirs. To qualify, individuals must be members of the decedent's family (as defined above) and meet both of the following qualifications:

1. They must also have been actively employed by the trade or business for at least 10 years prior to the date of death.
2. They must continue to materially participate in the trade or business for at least five years out of any eight-

year period within 10 years following the decedent's death.

Failure to comply with this second point will cause a scheduled pro rata recapture of the appropriate tax from all qualified heirs, not just the one in violation of the provisions. What that means, in plain English, is that if any heir doesn't keep working in the family business, it will cost the other members of the family. The IRS knows how to split heirs!

There are additional provisions and points to keep in mind. Here's one more: the business will fail to qualify for this special tax treatment if more than 35% of the adjusted ordinary gross income of the business for the year of the decedent's death was personal holding company income.

The details would fill another chapter. If this provision of the Taxpayer Relief Act of 1997 seems to apply to you, an estate planner can go through the details and help you get some additional relief.

4 WILLS AND OTHER WAYS

There's an old axiom: Where there's a will, there's a way. With a twist, that's true legally: a will is a way to dispose of your property. But it's not the only way. In this chapter we'll cover the essentials of a will and explore some ways to keep your assets out of probate.

■ WILLS

A will is to estate planning as notations are to music. It is but one of a complex combination of elements that, skillfully orchestrated, create a harmonious estate plan. Many people know that a will is an integral part of estate planning. They are correct, but planning involves much more.

Very few people really understand the entire scope of a will, how it is administered, and how it influences the distribution of estate assets after death. We'll give a brief overview of wills, discuss the essentials of a will, and provide an outline for a standard will.

By law, a "last will and testament" is a written document that directs how the testator's property is to be distributed when he or she dies. When that happens, the will is admitted to the probate court and established as a properly executed and valid will. The probate estate assets are then distributed. That's how it works, in general.

> ***Testator/Testatrix***—The man/woman who makes the will and whose estate is to be distributed.

ESSENTIALS OF A WILL

We usually think of a will as a document hammered out by an attorney and containing a lot of dry legal language punctuated by the frequent "inasmuch as" and "aforementioned" and "heretofore" and "notwithstanding." But a will can be valid even if not drawn up in this way. You'll want to check the laws of your particular state in this matter, as in all matters of estate planning.

But there are certain essentials to keep in mind when making a will that can stand up as valid:

- You must be of legal age. This means at least 18, but the age differs by state.
- You must be of sound mind and memory. What does that mean? That you understand what you're doing and that you know the general nature and extent of your property. That's known as "testamentary capacity." The law presumes mental competence; it's tough for anyone to challenge this point, if you make sure not to

neglect any major considerations and to at least mention the expected beneficiaries.

- You must put your will in writing. There are exceptions, but play it safe. It's best to have it typed or printed by a computer.
- You should identify yourself, by your legal name.
- You must include at least one substantive provision. That means that your will must actually dispose of your property and indicate that you intend the document to be a will.
- You must date your will. You should also specify where you're signing the will.
- You must sign the document, voluntarily. There are legal ways to get around this point, if you're unable to sign. It's also a good idea (and may be required by your state) to have some wording at the end to attest that this is your will.
- You must have three people witness your will who are not named as beneficiaries in the will. (Some states require only two witnesses.) The witnesses must watch you sign the document and they must know that it's your will, although they don't need to read it.

It's not very expensive to have an attorney draw up your will. A basic will can cost between $75 and $250. If you belong to a group legal service plan, you may be able to have a will drawn free of charge or at least for far less than the usual rate.

But there are also will kits that you can use. Check what requirements your particular state has for wills. You certainly don't want probate to decide that your quick 'n' easy will-in-a-box is not valid. You won't have a second chance to get it right.

Finally, the cheapest route is a statutory will, if authorized by law in your state. (They're legal in California, Maine, Michigan, New Mexico, and Wisconsin.) You can buy a statutory will in stationery stores for about $10. You won't get much for your money, since the forms are intended for simple needs. You can't change the wording, although you can modify them with codicils to add specific bequests.

All in all, your loved ones and your estate are probably worth investing a little more money to do your will up right. How would you feel if even one beneficiary lost out on what you intended to bequeath, simply because you cut corners on your will?

One final point here: an attorney can make sure that your will is legal and valid, but an estate planner can help you decide if it's good, if it will do what you want it to do—and how it fits with the rest of your planning.

Essentials of a Will

We can't provide you with a sample will that will meet your specific needs and prove valid in every state. But here's an outline of what's included in a typical will.

Introduction. This section gives the legal name and the residence of the testator, affirms that the testator/testatrix is of sound mind and memory, states that this is his or her last will and testament, and revokes any prior wills and codicils.

Typical wording:

"I, __name__, residing at __address__, being of sound mind and memory, declare this to be my last will and testament and I hereby revoke all prior wills and codicils."

(We'll cover codicils a little later.)

Liabilities. This section provides instructions for paying outstanding debts, funeral and administrative expenses, and any estate taxes.

Typical wording:

"I authorize my executor/executrix to pay my enforceable unsecured debts, medical and funeral expenses, costs incurred in administering my estate. These payments are to come from my residuary estate.

> *Residuary estate*—What remains of an estate after all specific property bequests have been made.

Specific devises. This section details any bequests of specific assets. It should identify each beneficiary fully by name and include alternate beneficiaries, in the event that a beneficiary has died or wishes to disclaim a bequest.

Typical wording:

"I bequeath all my personal effects and household items, such as jewelry, furniture, clothing, and books to my __relationship__, __name__. If he/she does not survive me or disclaims this property, I bequeath it to __relationship__, __name__.

"I bequeath my two cars and one truck to my __relationship__, __name__. If he/she does not survive me or disclaims this property, I bequeath it to __relationship__, __name__. ..."

> *Devise*—(as a noun) a bequest or gift in a will, (as a verb) to bequeath or give in a will.

Residuary estate. This section names a beneficiary or beneficiaries for what remains of the estate after the specific bequests.

Typical wording:

"I bequeath my residuary estate to my __relationship__, __name__. If he/she does not survive me or disclaims this property, I bequeath it to __relationship__, __name__."

Personal representative. This section names the person who will serve as executor or executrix and be responsible for executing the will. There should be a provision for an alternate.

Typical wording:

"I appoint my __relationship__, __name__, as executor/executrix of this will. If he/she is unwilling or unable to serve in this capacity, for any reason, I appoint my __relationship__, __name__ as successor executor/executrix. My executor/executrix shall have all the powers granted to executors under the laws of __state__ to exercise all legal powers as he/she determines to be in the best interests of my estate. I direct that no bond or security of any kind be required of my executor."

Signature. This section contains the signatures of the testator/testatrix and the witnesses, with the date and place of the signing.

Typical wording:

"I have signed this last will and testament in the presence of the undersigned witnesses on this day of _date_, _year_.

(signature)

"Signed and declared by _testator/testatrix_ to be his/her last will and testament, in our presence, who at his/her request, in his/her presence, and in the presence of each other have signed our names as witnesses."

Depending on your circumstances, you may want to add sections to do any of the following:

- Appoint a guardian for any minor children
- Instruct the executor or executrix to set up an account for the children under the Uniform Gifts to Minors Act or the Uniform Transfers to Minors Act
- Forgive certain debts
- Disinherit one or all of your children

> ***Uniform Gifts to Minors Act/Uniform Transfers to Minors Act***—Law that allows an account to be set up for a minor, with an adult designated as custodian of the property for the minor, who is the legal owner of the property and has an unrestricted right to it upon reaching the age of majority (18 to 21, depending on the state).

Final Details

Some wills also include instructions regarding funeral arrangements and burial wishes. But some experts advise against including these matters in a will, since it might not be examined until days after a death, by which time other arrangements may have been made.

You should play it safe and express any funeral or burial wishes in advance to your loved ones or to anyone who might be in a position to make the arrangements. It's wisest to write out the details and make copies for these people.

The best way is in what's called a *letter of instructions.* This is a memo of personal details that you should keep with your will. Send a copy to your executor. Keep one for yourself. The letter of instructions should include such information as the location of your will, the location of other vital documents, and any wishes for your funeral and burial. It costs so little to make sure that people know what you want. It also will help them make decisions at a time that will be very difficult for them emotionally.

> *Letter of instructions*—A memo that contains such information as the location of your will, the location of other vital documents, and any wishes for your funeral and burial.

So, once you've got a will, where do you put it? The usual reaction is to treat it as you treat all of your important documents and put in a safe-deposit box. If you do that, remember that the bank might seal the box when you die. When that happens, the box can be opened only when a release is obtained. So keep several copies where they'll be accessible: the person whom you've named as executor of your will should have a copy, of course, as well as your attorney and members of your family.

Changes, Changes, Changes...

We all know that there's nothing certain in life but changes. In fact, as soon as you make out your will, the odds are really good that something in your life will change. You may acquire more assets or get rid of some. People may enter your life whom you want to include among your beneficiaries—e.g., a grandchild is born or a child marries. You may lose a beneficiary—e.g., somebody dies, a charitable organization shuts down, or you decide to disinherit a relative or a former friend.

So, then, is it back to the will-drawing board? Not necessarily.

You can amend your will by adding a codicil. You simply specify the change that you'd like to make, following the same legal procedures as for your will: put it in writing, date it, and sign it with witnesses.

> ***Codicil***—A legal change to a will, written and properly witnessed.

Because of the formalities involved in making valid codicils and because it's so easy to prepare wills now, it may be better simply to prepare a new will. You'd certainly be wise to do so if the change is major, such as disinheriting a child or changing executors.

One final word here: ademption. That's a legal term from a Latin word meaning "taking away." This is when you take away something from your estate, when you dispose of property that you bequeathed in your will, so that the bequest is invalidated.

> ***Ademption***—The removal of property from an estate by the owner after he or she has bequeathed it in a will.

Here's an example. You draw up your will and leave to your favorite niece that 1955 Rolls-Royce Silver Dawn that she's loved since she was two. But then, a few years later, you run into a sudden liquidity problem, so you sell the Silver Dawn. Three months after that, you come into a little money, so you immediately go out and buy a 1959 Rolls-Royce Phantom V. After all, your niece probably won't know the difference. Ah, but she will—because that Phantom won't go to your niece, since it's not the vehicle that you specified in your will.

Our advice here is to anticipate changes, then prepare for them. If you provide in your will to leave a specific piece of property, you might want to include a provision that would cover the possibility of selling or exchanging the property.

Intestate: The Slow Route Through Probate

The term "intestate" describes a person who dies without leaving a will. A person who dies without a will creates the very real potential for assets to be distributed in ways that he or she never intended. If you don't express your wishes in a will, you're leaving it to state law to write your will for you. And for your loved ones, that may be a most unfortunate, time-consuming, and expensive mistake.

> ***Intestate***—The state of having died without leaving a will.

Intestacy creates the worst possible situation: the distribution of every piece of probate property in the estate must be decided through probate. The best situation, in contrast, would be to avoid probate altogether. In recent times there has been much information distributed on methods of doing so. We'll discuss these methods later in this chapter.

You understand why it's a very bad idea to leave to probate all the decisions about your estate. But why do people want to avoid the probate process entirely? The most common incentives for avoiding probate are that the process takes time, costs money, and is a public procedure subject to anyone's inspection at the county courthouse. We will now consider these issues in more detail.

■ PROBATE

What is probate? The word comes from the Latin, probare, meaning "to prove." It's a legal procedure, supervised by the court, to prove a will is valid. That's essentially all that probate needs to be—assuming that there's a will. If not, as we've stressed, probate makes up for that missing document of closure.

> ***Probate***—The legal procedure to determine, if there's a will, whether the will is valid or, if there's no will, how the estate should be distributed.

That's the concept of probate. But, of course, things are always more complicated in practice.

THE PROBATE PROCESS: USUAL SCENARIOS

The probate process gathers all the assets in the estate, takes out whatever is needed to pay debts and taxes and administrative expenses, and then distributes the assets among the beneficiaries. That process can take time, cost a little or a lot, and open up your life to anybody with an interest or just idle curiosity.

Time. Generally, the probate process will take from four months to two years. It can take even longer. How long it takes to settle an estate is determined by the following factors:

- Whether there's a valid will
- What types of assets make up the estate
- How well the estate's assets are organized
- Whether there are trusts
- Whether the probate process is formal or informal
- How competent the executor is
- How many beneficiaries there are
- How easily the beneficiaries can be located

When it's necessary to liquidate property, that process takes time, particularly with real estate, business assets, or unique property (unlike publicly traded stock).

Another possible time factor is challenges. Wills can also be challenged by neglected potential heirs or dissatisfied beneficiaries, who may disagree with distribution or even raise the question of testamentary capacity.

Cost. The cost of probate is difficult to predetermine, as it is affected by many of the same influences mentioned above. Another factor is the probate laws for the particular state.

Probate costs rise as the complications multiply. Some states have unique statutory probate processes that tend to inflate costs. Minnesota has adopted the Uniform Probate Code, which facilitates the process and minimizes costs—if an estate is properly planned for distribution. South Dakota has also adopted the Uniform Probate Code, but not Wisconsin, Iowa, or North Dakota.

Publicity. Probate court documents are public records. Anyone who wants to research a probate estate's records can simply go to the courthouse for that information.

Does that matter to you? Maybe. Maybe not. But it's something to keep in mind if there's any information about your estate that you'd like to keep confidential. If ongoing business or personal issues warrant, you should consider strategies that will keep some or all of your estate out of probate, to ensure privacy.

OK. That's a quick description of how probate works for people who die testate, that is, with a will. It gets a whole lot worse if there's no will.

> ***Testate***—The state of having died with a will.

The Probate Process: Worst-Case Scenarios

When a person dies intestate, the probate process must also, in essence, make a will after the fact. Here again, what happens depends to some extent on the particular state.

State law will determine what happens to your property. (This process is called "intestate succession.") Your property will be distributed to your spouse and children or, if you have neither, to other relatives according to a statutory formula. If no relatives can be found to inherit your property, it will go into your state's coffers. Also, in the absence of a will, a court will determine who will care for your young children and their property if the other parent is unavailable or unfit.

> ***Intestate succession***—The process for determining what will happen to the property and any minor children of a person who dies without a will.

You can consult the probate code for your state to find out the line of intestate succession. You can also consult with an attorney. But first, you should answer this question: Why put any effort into knowing how a probate court is likely to distribute your property if you can take action to keep that important matter out of the hands of strangers?

Do we dare emphasize yet again that dying without a will creates a scenario in which your assets may be distributed in ways that you never intended? We hope that, at this point, you are determined to make out a will—and interested in exploring ways to make sure that at least some of your property will bypass the probate process.

■ BYPASSING PROBATE

There are ways to keep property from passing through probate. First, we'll discuss how certain types of assets and certain types of titling allow us to bypass probate entirely.

As we noted earlier, a will distributes assets within a person's probate estate. Many times testators expect that their wills are going to take care of distributing all their assets, but they would later roll over in their graves as their wills fail to do as expected. Why? Because of the type of assets or how they are owned.

Types of Assets

Certain types of assets by their very nature rarely end up being subject to probate, as we will discuss.

Asset types fall into several main categories:

- Real estate
- Stocks and bonds
- Mutual funds
- Bank accounts
- Annuities
- Life insurance
- Individual Retirement Accounts (IRAs)
- 401(k) plans
- Profit-sharing plans
- Pensions
- Miscellaneous tax-qualified retirement plans
- Personal property

The type of asset will determine what titling choices are available, that is, the ways in which an asset may be owned. How an asset is titled will determine whether an asset can be distributed without a will and thus avoid probate.

> *Titling*—Ownership of an asset, usually as individual owner, joint tenants, or tenants in common.

Figure 4a shows how the asset classes listed above can be owned and whether or not the assets will be included among the probate assets.

■ TYPES OF OWNERSHIP

Figure 4a shows three types of ownership: individual ownership, joint tenancy, and tenancy in common. These are the most common methods of titling used. Certain titling of ownership passes assets outside of probate directly to the beneficiary or joint owner. In this section, we will explore ownership titling and how it affects estate distribution.

Individual ownership. This is, as you would expect, when only one person owns the property. Individual ownership generally allows for distribution by will. Examples could include real estate, securities, bank accounts.

Joint tenancy and joint tenancy with right of survivor. These are the most

Type of Ownership Generally Available And If Typically Subject To Probate

	Individual Ownership	Tenants In Common	Joint Tenancy	Probate Avoidance Available*	Probate Assets**
Real Estate	Yes	Yes	Yes	Yes (4)	Yes
Stocks & Bonds	Yes	Yes	Yes	Yes (5)	Yes
Mutual Funds	Yes	Yes	Yes	Yes (5)	Yes
Bank Accounts	Yes	Yes	Yes	Yes (6)	Yes
Annuities	Yes (1)	Yes (2)	Yes (3)	Yes	No
Life Insurance	Yes (1)	Yes (2)	Yes (3)	Yes	No
IRA's	Yes (1)	No	No	Yes	No
401K's	Yes (1)	No	No	Yes	No
Profit Sharing	Yes (1)	No	No	Yes	No
Pensions	Yes (1)	No	No	Yes	No
Personal Property	Yes	No	Yes	Yes (7)	Yes

Key:

(1) Assets typically owned by Individual. Non-probate beneficiary designation available.

(2) Non-qualified annuities and life insurance may, in some instances, be held as Tenancy-In-Common.

(3) Non-qualified annuities and life insurance may, in some instances, be held in Joint Tenancy.

(4) Real estate may be held in life estate, or a quit claim deed can be executed during lifetime.

(5) Mutual funds, stocks, bonds, and securities can have transfer on death designations.

(6) Bank accounts may have a payable on death or Totten Trust designation.

(7) A will can authorize preparations of a list to handle distribution of personal property.

* The ability to name a beneficiary and avoid probate.

** Assets typically subject to probate if owned Individually or as Tenancy-In-Common, or if the "estate" is beneficiary.

FIGURE 4A

common types of asset ownership between husband and wife. When one of the joint tenants dies, his or her interest passes to the surviving spouse automatically. This type of titling does not allow for distribution by will. This is only logical, because these two types of ownership are joint. There is no probate requirement.

> *Joint tenants in common*—Owners of a shared asset, with the interest of any owner, upon death, becoming part of that person's estate.

> *Joint tenants with rights of survivorship*—Owners of a shared asset, with the interest of any owner, upon death, passing to the surviving co-owners.

This titling may seem attractive, but it can have adverse consequences for estate planning. However, for many estates it is an appropriate form of titling.

Tenancy in common. This titling allows individuals undivided interest in assets to be distributed by a will. As with joint tenancy, two or more individuals are on the title of the asset. Although this type of titling is available for many assets, it is most commonly used for real estate.

Titling can be particularly important if you live in a community property state (Arizona, California, Louisiana, Nevada, New Mexico, Texas, Washington, and Wisconsin). The laws in these states provide that most property acquired during marriage is held equally by husband and wife. There are exceptions, notably property acquired by inheritance or as a gift. It's wise to settle possible questions of ownership before the time comes to settle your estate.

Ownership of assets has a significant impact on how well an estate plan will work and what impact the will may have when the estate is settled. Questions of ownership can be quite confusing.

People may ask themselves, "Just what does my will do for me?" The answer: A will distributes only assets that are in your probate estate.

Estate planning for distribution of assets is very involved. It depends a great deal on asset titling.

What about those assets that don't end up in a probate estate? How are they easily recognized? The assets that do not typically end up in a probate estate include life insurance, annuities, retirement plans (such as IRAs, 401ks, profit sharing, pensions, and tax-sheltered accounts) and assets owned in joint tenancy. With the exception of joint tenancy, which transfers title to the surviving joint tenant(s), all of these types of assets provide for a beneficiary designation that allows for distribution without going through probate.

■ LIFE ESTATE

A life estate is an additional type of ownership that avoids probate. It is actually a lifetime transfer, but the person making the transfer, the life tenant, retains all use of the property. In most cases, the life tenant cannot sell or mortgage the property without the permission of the specified new owner, called the remainderman.

> ***Life tenant***—A person who makes a lifetime transfer of a property and retains all use of the property for life.
>
> ***Remainderman***—A person who has a future interest in a life estate or a trust.

A typical use of this titling is parents transfer real estate to their children while reserving the right to use the property until death. A life estate can also be used by a person to provide a home for his or her grandparents as life tenants; the home would then pass to his or her children when the grandparents die.

Since the life estate is an actual lifetime transfer of title, the property is not subject to probate and a will has no impact on it, since the life tenant is no longer the owner. However, the value of the property is included in the estate of the life tenant for estate tax purposes.

Life estate is a simple, very effective tool in estate planning. But, as with all estate planning techniques, you should analyze it carefully and compare it against other strategies.

■ TRUSTS: ANOTHER WAY TO AVOID PROBATE

Finally, we conclude our discussion of wills and probate by noting that several types of trusts allow you to bypass probate. But that's only one advantage of trusts. We'll discuss the various types of trusts and their advantages in Chapter 6, "How to Use Trusts in Estate Planning."

5 Planning for Liquidity

Let's talk *liquidity.* That's just a fancy word for the ease with which an asset can be turned into cash. Cash is liquid because we can use it for almost every sort of economic need or interest. (Of course, if you were in the middle of a desert, for example, you might not be able to trade cash for water—a real liquid. But in almost any situation, cash is liquidity to the extreme.)

> ***Liquidity***—The degree to which an asset can be converted into cash quickly and without loss of value.

■ Degrees of Liquidity

We distinguish between liquid assets and non-liquid or illiquid assets, but that's a simplification. Liquidity is usually relative, depending on the situation. If you can sell an asset for a fair price or even better in little or no time, then that asset is liquid. If, on the other hand, it takes a long time to sell an asset at a fair price, that asset is not very liquid. So, when we use the terms "liquid" and "non-liquid" or "illiquid" or "fixed," we're really discussing areas along a continuum.

Assets that are liquid, besides cash, would range from bank accounts (savings or checking) and certificates of deposit to investments such as savings bonds, Treasury Bills, money market funds, mutual funds, stocks, and municipal bonds or municipal bond mutual funds. Keep in mind that differences exist among liquid assets. For example, unlike bank accounts, if you suddenly had to redeem your shares in a mutual fund—even a money market mutual fund—your shares might be worth more or less than you paid for them. Assets that are not very liquid would include real estate, motor vehicles, collectibles, personal property, thinly traded securities, and closely held stock (stock in a company owned by family members or a small group of individuals but usually not the general public).

Estates often consist primarily of non-liquid assets. That's normal, because our lives are full of assets of various degrees of liquidity. That's not a problem, unless there's a financial emergency. (Quick! How much cash could you get together within 24 hours?)

Death brings urgency to our economic state. Often there's a cash crunch immediately following a death: assets, assets everywhere, but not enough liquid. There are sudden financial needs—at a time when it can be very difficult to make prudent decisions about finding the cash to meet those needs.

Sure, you can sell assets at prices that will guarantee liquidity—if you don't mind losing a lot of value just to make a quick sale. (We're all familiar with liquidation sales: they're quite a bargain if you're buying, but for the people selling the goods the losses can be huge.)

Because of the sudden need for cash, planning for sufficient estate liquidity is critical in many business situations and prudent when trying to prevent an estate from shrinking. After all, if you're not forced to convert assets to cash immediately, you're far more likely to get a good price for them—if you decide to sell.

Sufficient estate liquidity also means that selling will be a choice, not an economic necessity. So your spouse will be able to keep the house and your children will be able to fight over the keys to your car—if you plan for estate liquidity.

■ PLANNING FOR LIQUIDITY

The proper planning should ensure that your estate will have enough cash available to meet all the estate planning needs and provide adequate estate liquidity. But what's "adequate"?

To decide what's adequate in your particular situation, take the following steps:

1. Determine potential needs.
2. Assign a realistic value to the needs.
3. Examine the resources that can be used.

Determine Your Potential Needs

First you've got to anticipate the financial demands that your estate is likely to face. An estate may need liquidity to meet any or all of the following needs:

- To pay debts
- To settle creditor claims
- To pay probate and administrative expenses
- To pay funeral and burial expenses
- To cover the income needs of family members
- To pay income and estate taxes
- To ensure smooth transition of business interests
- To execute buy/sell agreements

> ***Buy/sell agreement***—The most common way to transfer ownership of a business when a partner dies: all partners in a business agree to purchase the interest of any partner who dies.

Calculate the Costs of Your Needs

Which estate needs should you plan to cover? List those needs. And how much do you expect each to cost your estate? You may want to make a few phone calls to get those figures.

As you calculate potential costs, you should bear in mind the probable effect of inflation. If you're an optimist, you might want to assume a rate of 3% or 4%. If you're the type who worries a lot, use a higher figure. Then add up all of those projected costs. That total is your liquidity deficiency.

Examine Your Resources

Maybe you've got a pot of cash somewhere that will cover your liquidity deficiency. In that case, congratulations! You can skip on to the next chapter.

If not, then you definitely need to read this next section. To cover your deficiency, we're going to discuss the following common approaches to ensuring estate liquidity:

- Creating a specific savings fund
- Using operating cash on hand
- Selling off assets
- Mortgaging or borrowing
- Using life insurance proceeds

CREATING A SPECIFIC SAVINGS FUND

Creating a savings fund for estate liquidity requires significant lead time. Let's assume that you establish an account to provide funding for a buy/sell agreement with a target need of $300,000. Your investments allow you to earn an after-tax return of 6% and your cash flow allows you to invest $20,000 annually. How long will it take to fund the buy/sell account? Just a little over 11 years.

(If you want to go through those years one by one and evaluate the progress of your fund, see Figure 5a.)

Now, what if the need is $1,000,000 and you still allocate $20,000 annually? How long will it take to reach your goal? To make a cool mil, it will take 23 years and nine months.

Analysis Of Special Savings Fund

Year	Projected Deposits Annually (a)	Projected Increase At 6% Net(b)	Total Fund Annually (c)	Fund Goal $300,000 Shortage (d)
1	$20,000	$0	$20,000	($280,000)
2	$20,000	$1,200	$41,200	($258,800)
3	$20,000	$2,472	$63,672	($236,328)
4	$20,000	$3,820	$87,492	($212,508)
5	$20,000	$5,250	$112,742	($187,258)
6	$20,000	$6,765	$139,506	($160,494)
7	$20,000	$8,370	$167,877	($132,123)
8	$20,000	$10,073	$197,949	($102,051)
9	$20,000	$11,877	$229,826	($70,174)
10	$20,000	$13,790	$263,616	($36,384)
11	$20,000	$15,817	$299,433	($567)

Key:

(a) $20,000 annually deposited in to special savings fund.

(b) Assumed rate of return 6% after taxes.

(c) Accumulation of fund including growth.

(d) Projected shortage of fund versus goal.

FIGURE 5A

Analysis Of Special Savings Fund

Year	Projected Deposits Annually (a)	Projected Increase At 6% Net(b)	Total Fund Annually (c)	Fund Goal $1,000,000 Shortage (d)
1	$20,000	$0	$20,000	($980,000)
2	$20,000	$1,200	$41,200	($958,800)
3	$20,000	$2,472	$63,672	($936,328)
4	$20,000	$3,820	$87,492	($912,508)
5	$20,000	$5,250	$112,742	($887,258)
6	$20,000	$6,765	$139,506	($860,494)
7	$20,000	$8,370	$167,877	($832,123)
8	$20,000	$10,073	$197,949	($802,051)
9	$20,000	$11,877	$229,826	($770,174)
10	$20,000	$13,790	$263,616	($736,384)
11	$20,000	$15,817	$299,433	($700,567)
12	$20,000	$17,966	$337,399	($662,601)
13	$20,000	$20,244	$377,643	($622,357)
14	$20,000	$22,659	$420,301	($579,699)
15	$20,000	$25,218	$465,519	($534,481)
16	$20,000	$27,931	$513,451	($486,549)
17	$20,000	$30,807	$564,258	($435,742)
18	$20,000	$33,855	$618,113	($381,887)
19	$20,000	$37,087	$675,200	($324,800)
20	$20,000	$40,512	$735,712	($264,288)
21	$20,000	$44,143	$799,855	($200,145)
22	$20,000	$47,991	$867,846	($132,154)
23	$20,000	$52,071	$939,917	($60,083)
24	$20,000	$56,395	$1,016,312	$16,312

Key:

(a) $20,000 annually deposited in to special savings fund.

(b) Assumed rate of return 6% after taxes.

(c) Accumulation of fund including growth.

(d) Projected shortage of fund versus goal.

FIGURE 5B

(Figure 5b shows the annual increments for each one of those years.)

We've got to ask a very delicate question here: How much time do you have? Maybe you've got 11 years. Maybe you've got 23 years and nine months. You could have many, many more years than that. But, as we all know, any of us could die at any given moment.

If you evaluate this approach to liquidity, it could make good sense in terms of time and money—in theory. But if you want certainty, never count on time being on your side.

Using Operating Cash on Hand

In most business situations, using operating cash on hand is only a short-term solution. It's usually not long before the appropriation adversely affects the business. You should not count on cash on hand to do more than buy a little time before a permanent solution can be arranged.

In personal situations, cash on hand typically is not adequate to meet estate liquidity needs. Let's consider a variation on that question we asked at the beginning of this chapter: How much cash could your executor get together to settle the estate without losing too much value? Would that amount take care of the needs?

Selling Off Assets

Quite often, the executor of a will may meet the need for liquidity by selling off some assets. The liquidation of assets can be handled in three ways.

If your executor decides to sell personal or business assets that do not have a ready market, he or she will likely be offering those assets to the public at an estate auction or estate sale. That means those assets will probably sell at less than their value, perhaps far less. (What's your first reaction when you're driving or walking down a street and you notice an "Estate Sale" sign? An opportunity to get some bargains, right?)

Your executor may decide to sell at least some assets separately. That should allow him or her to negotiate some better selling. But if the buyers know the reason for the sale, the circumstances may lead them to offer less money than your assets might otherwise have commanded.

Investments may be the best choice for liquidity. Your executor could sell at least certain investments anonymously, so the estate may not lose any of their value. But then the beneficiaries of your will would not enjoy the appreciation on those investments that you were careful to choose and hold.

Obviously this whole area of raising liquidity is a matter that you should discuss with the person you've named to execute your will. Discuss your assets, and then decide what might be best to sell to cover any liquidity deficiency and how the sales might be handled best.

Then crunch the numbers. How much cash could be raised quickly? Would that amount be sufficient to cover the needs of your estate?

Mortgaging or Borrowing

A common solution for estate liquidity problems is to mortgage or borrow. Unfortunately, this can be difficult.

In a business situation, it often means borrowing money after the person with the greatest expertise to make money and repay debt is gone. In a personal situation, this is usually a time when taking on more debt is the last thing the survivors want to do.

How much debt might your loved ones or partners incur to provide the necessary liquidity? For the sake of example, let's take two figures.

If they needed $300,000 and could borrow that amount at 9% interest, over a 20-year repayment period it

Analysis Of Borrowing $300,000 for 20 Years

Year	Annual Interest Rate 9.00%	Annual Debt Payment	Balance Outstanding Debt	Cumulative Interest Expense (Not Tax-Adjusted)
1	$27,000	$32,864	$294,136	$27,000
2	$26,472	$32,864	$287,744	$53,472
3	$25,897	$32,864	$280,777	$79,369
4	$25,270	$32,864	$273,183	$104,639
5	$24,586	$32,864	$264,906	$129,226
6	$23,842	$32,864	$255,883	$153,067
7	$23,029	$32,864	$246,049	$176,097
8	$22,144	$32,864	$235,329	$198,241
9	$21,180	$32,864	$223,645	$219,421
10	$20,128	$32,864	$210,909	$239,549
11	$18,982	$32,864	$197,026	$258,530
12	$17,732	$32,864	$181,895	$276,263
13	$16,371	$32,864	$165,401	$292,633
14	$14,886	$32,864	$147,423	$307,519
15	$13,268	$32,864	$127,828	$320,788
16	$11,504	$32,864	$106,468	$332,292
17	$9,582	$32,864	$83,186	$341,874
18	$7,487	$32,864	$57,809	$349,361
19	$5,203	$32,864	$30,148	$354,564
20	$2,713	$32,864	($3)	$357,277

Total Payment: $657,280
(Principal and Interest)

FIGURE 5C

would then cost $657,280 (Figure 5c). If they needed $1,000,000 and could borrow that amount at 9% interest, over a 20-year repayment period it would cost them $2,190,940 (Figure 5d).

Using Life Insurance Proceeds

Life insurance proceeds are without a doubt the very best way to fund estate liquidity. Why?

Analysis Of Borrowing $1,000,000 for 20 Years

Year	Annual Interest Rate 9.00%	Annual Debt Payment	Balance Outstanding Debt	Cumulative Interest Expense (Not Tax-Adjusted)
1	$90,000	$109,547	$980,453	$90,000
2	$88,241	$109,547	$959,147	$178,241
3	$86,323	$109,547	$935,923	$264,564
4	$84,233	$109,547	$910,609	$348,797
5	$81,955	$109,547	$883,017	$430,752
6	$79,472	$109,547	$852,941	$510,223
7	$76,765	$109,547	$820,159	$586,988
8	$73,814	$109,547	$784,426	$660,802
9	$70,598	$109,547	$745,478	$731,401
10	$67,093	$109,547	$703,024	$798,494
11	$63,272	$109,547	$656,749	$861,766
12	$59,107	$109,547	$606,309	$920,873
13	$54,568	$109,547	$551,330	$975,441
14	$49,620	$109,547	$491,403	$1,025,061
15	$44,226	$109,547	$426,082	$1,069,287
16	$38,347	$109,547	$354,883	$1,107,635
17	$31,939	$109,547	$277,275	$1,139,574
18	$24,955	$109,547	$192,683	$1,164,529
19	$17,341	$109,547	$100,477	$1,181,870
20	$9,043	$109,547	($27)	$1,190,913

Total Payment: $2,190,940
(Principal and Interest)

Figure 5D

Analysis Of Life Insurance Estate Liquidity Requirement $300,000 Funding For Male Age 65, Assumed Policy Rate 6.5% *

Year	Age	Annual Payments To Policy (a)	Cash Value Build-Up (b)	Face Value Of Life Insurance (c)	Annual Loan Payment (d)	Annual Savings Payment (e)
1	65	$14,000	$10,080	$300,000	$32,864	$20,000
2	66	$14,000	na	$300,000	$32,864	$20,000
3	67	$14,000	na	$300,000	$32,864	$20,000
4	68	$14,000	na	$300,000	$32,864	$20,000
5	69	$14,000	$58,973	$300,000	$32,864	$20,000
6	70	$14,000	na	$300,000	$32,864	$20,000
7	71	$14,000	na	$300,000	$32,864	$20,000
8	72	$14,000	na	$300,000	$32,864	$20,000
9	73	$14,000	na	$300,000	$32,864	$20,000
10	74	$14,000	$185,495	$300,000	$32,864	$20,000
11	75	$0	na	$300,000	$32,864	$20,000
12	76	$0	na	$300,000	$32,864	$0
13	77	$0	na	$300,000	$32,864	$0
14	78	$0	na	$300,000	$32,864	$0
15	79	$0	$185,495	$300,000	$32,864	$0
16	80	$0	na	$300,000	$32,864	$0
17	81	$0	na	$300,000	$32,864	$0
18	82	$0	na	$300,000	$32,864	$0
19	83	$0	na	$300,000	$32,864	$0
20	84	$0	$228,768	$300,000	$32,864	$0
21	85	$0	na	$300,000	$0	$0
26	90	$0	$295,374	$300,000	$0	$0
31	95	$0	$396,487	$396,487	$0	$0
36	100	$0	$538,843	$538,843	$0	$0
		Insurance	Total Costs Of Funding		Borrowing	Saving
		$140,000	For $300,000		$657,280	$220,000

Key:

(a) Annual contributions to life insurance contract.

(b) Annual projected build-up of cash value in insurance contract.

(c) Available cash in the event of death of the insured (death benefit).

(d) Annual outlay savings.

(e) Annual outlay borrowing.

* Major national insurance company illustration (policy provides 16 year guarantee at illustrated premium).

FIGURE 5E

Analysis Of Life Insurance Estate Liquidity Requirement $1,000,000 Funding For Male Age 65, Assumed Policy Rate 6.5% *

Year	Age	Annual Payments To Policy (a)	Cash Value Build-Up (b)	Face Value Of Life Insurance (c)	Annual Loan Payment (d)	Annual Savings Payment (e)
1	65	$42,500	$29,498	$1,000,000	$109,547	$20,000
2	66	$42,500	na	$1,000,000	$109,547	$20,000
3	67	$42,500	na	$1,000,000	$109,547	$20,000
4	68	$42,500	na	$1,000,000	$109,547	$20,000
5	69	$42,500	$172,569	$1,000,000	$109,547	$20,000
6	70	$42,500	na	$1,000,000	$109,547	$20,000
7	71	$42,500	na	$1,000,000	$109,547	$20,000
8	72	$42,500	na	$1,000,000	$109,547	$20,000
9	73	$42,500	na	$1,000,000	$109,547	$20,000
10	74	$42,500	$424,495	$1,000,000	$109,547	$20,000
11	75	$0	na	$1,000,000	$109,547	$20,000
12	76	$0	na	$1,000,000	$109,547	$20,000
13	77	$0	na	$1,000,000	$109,547	$20,000
14	78	$0	na	$1,000,000	$109,547	$20,000
15	79	$0	$533,475	$1,000,000	$109,547	$20,000
16	80	$0	na	$1,000,000	$109,547	$20,000
17	81	$0	na	$1,000,000	$109,547	$20,000
18	82	$0	na	$1,000,000	$109,547	$20,000
19	83	$0	na	$1,000,000	$109,547	$20,000
20	84	$0	$621,281	$1,000,000	$109,547	$20,000
21	85	$0	na	$1,000,000	$0	$20,000
26	90	$0	$721,040	$1,000,000	$0	$0
31	95	$0	$863,077	$1,000,000	$0	$0
36	100	$0	$1,141,979	$1,141,979	$0	$0

	Insurance	Total Costs Of Funding For $1,000,000	Borrowing	Saving
	$425,000		$2,190,940	$480,000

Key:

(a) Annual contributions to life insurance contract.

(b) Annual projected build-up of cash value in insurance contract.

(c) Available cash in the event of death of the insured (death benefit).

(d) Annual outlay savings.

(e) Annual outlay borrowing.

* Major national insurance company illustration (policy provides 15 year guarantee at illustrated premium).

FIGURE 5F

For two very good reasons:

- Life insurance provides proceeds when they're needed, regardless of how much time has elapsed.
- Life insurance typically costs less to fund than any other method of ensuring liquidity.

Figures 5e and 5f show how a life insurance policy can provide liquidity in our two example amounts, $300,000 and $1,000,000.

There may be a disadvantage, however, in depending on life insurance. To take out a policy requires moderately good health. In the past, that requirement may have put this strategy out of reach for some people.

But a relatively recent creation has improved this situation for married people—survivorship life insurance. Also known as joint, joint survivorship, two-life or second-to-die, this type of policy was first developed in 1961, but gained popularity with the passing of the Economic Recovery Tax Act of 1981.

Survivorship life insurance is a single policy that insures two lives, usually spouses, and pays off only upon the death of the second person. In some instances, only one person must be insurable for both to qualify for a survivorship policy. This type of life insurance may be especially useful in estate planning by families where one person has serious health problems.

> ***Survivorship life insurance***—A life insurance policy that covers two people, usually spouses, and pays off only when the second person dies. Also known as joint life, two-life, or second-to-die.

Survivorship insurance not only allows coverage for people who might have trouble getting conventional life insurance, but it also can provide coverage for less expense.

Premium rates are based on the joint life expectancy of the two persons, so for a given face value the premium rate is lower than it would be for either person individually. A survivorship policy for $1,000,000 costs less than a conventional $1,000,000 policy on one person or two separate $500,000 policies. Survivorship life insurance is available as whole, universal, variable, or combinations.

Figures 5g and 5h show how a survivorship life insurance policy can provide liquidity in our two example amounts, $300,000 and $1,000,000.

So, the best way to ensure estate liquidity is through life insurance—conventional or survivorship. However, life insurance should not have your estate named as the beneficiary. This action will guarantee probate and tie up the proceeds when they are needed. Life insurance does not have to be a probate asset. By naming your business partner, your spouse, your loved ones, etc., as beneficiary of your life insurance contract, probate has been avoided and the proceeds are available immediately for the intended purpose.

The bottom line is that, with careful planning to reduce estate taxes and probate expenses and a life insurance policy to cover your estate liquidity needs, you can pass your estate intact to your heirs.

Analysis Of Life Insurance Estate Liquidity Requirement $300,000 Funding For Two Lives Male And Female Age 65, Assumed Policy Rate 6.85%*

Year	Age	Annual Payments To Policy (a)	Cash Value Build-Up (b)	Face Value Of Life Insurance (c)	Annual Loan Payment (d)	Annual Savings Payment (e)
1	65	$10,000	$7,626	$300,000	$32,864	$20,000
2	66	$10,000	na	$300,000	$32,864	$20,000
3	67	$10,000	na	$300,000	$32,864	$20,000
4	68	$10,000	na	$300,000	$32,864	$20,000
5	69	$10,000	$42,261	$300,000	$32,864	$20,000
6	70	$10,000	na	$300,000	$32,864	$20,000
7	71	$10,000	na	$300,000	$32,864	$20,000
8	72	$10,000	na	$300,000	$32,864	$20,000
9	73	$10,000	na	$300,000	$32,864	$20,000
10	74	$10,000	$108,304	$300,000	$32,864	$20,000
11	75	$0	na	$300,000	$32,864	$20,000
12	76	$0	na	$300,000	$32,864	$0
13	77	$0	na	$300,000	$32,864	$0
14	78	$0	na	$300,000	$32,864	$0
15	79	$0	$135,423	$300,000	$32,864	$0
16	80	$0	na	$300,000	$32,864	$0
17	81	$0	na	$300,000	$32,864	$0
18	82	$0	na	$300,000	$32,864	$0
19	83	$0	na	$300,000	$32,864	$0
20	84	$0	$171,945	$300,000	$32,864	$0
21	85	$0	na	$300,000	$0	$0
26	90	$0	$226,654	$300,000	$0	$0
31	95	$0	$316,411	$316,411	$0	$0
36	100	$0	$454,302	$454,302	$0	$0

	Insurance	Total Costs Of Funding	Borrowing	Saving
	$100,000	For $300,000	$657,280	$220,000

Key:

(a) Annual contributions to life insurance contract.

(b) Annual projected build-up of cash value in insurance contract.

(c) Available cash in the event of death of the insured (death benefit).

(d) Annual outlay savings.

(e) Annual outlay borrowing.

* Major national insurance company illustration (policy provides 19 year guarantee at illustrated premium).

FIGURE 5G

Analysis Of Life Insurance Estate Liquidity Requirement $1,000,000 Funding For Two Lives Male And Female Age 65, Assumed Policy Rate 6.85%*

Year	Age	Annual Payments To Policy (a)	Cash Value Build-Up (b)	Face Value Of Life Insurance (c)	Annual Loan Payment (d)	Annual Savings Payment (e)
1	65	$30,000	$22,271	$1,000,000	$109,547	$20,000
2	66	$30,000	na	$1,000,000	$109,547	$20,000
3	67	$30,000	na	$1,000,000	$109,547	$20,000
4	68	$30,000	na	$1,000,000	$109,547	$20,000
5	69	$30,000	$122,725	$1,000,000	$109,547	$20,000
6	70	$30,000	na	$1,000,000	$109,547	$20,000
7	71	$30,000	na	$1,000,000	$109,547	$20,000
8	72	$30,000	na	$1,000,000	$109,547	$20,000
9	73	$30,000	na	$1,000,000	$109,547	$20,000
10	74	$30,000	$316,617	$1,000,000	$109,547	$20,000
11	75	$0	na	$1,000,000	$109,547	$20,000
12	76	$0	na	$1,000,000	$109,547	$20,000
13	77	$0	na	$1,000,000	$109,547	$20,000
14	78	$0	na	$1,000,000	$109,547	$20,000
15	79	$0	$384,159	$1,000,000	$109,547	$20,000
16	80	$0	na	$1,000,000	$109,547	$20,000
17	81	$0	na	$1,000,000	$109,547	$20,000
18	82	$0	na	$1,000,000	$109,547	$20,000
19	83	$0	na	$1,000,000	$109,547	$20,000
20	84	$0	$465,276	$1,000,000	$109,547	$20,000
21	85	$0	na	$1,000,000	$0	$20,000
26	90	$0	$576,098	$1,000,000	$0	$0
31	95	$0	$747,260	$1,000,000	$0	$0
36	100	$0	$1,036,870	$1,036,870	$0	$0

	Insurance	Total Costs Of Funding	Borrowing	Saving
	$300,000	For $1,000,000	$2,190,940	$480,000

Key:
(a) Annual contributions to life insurance contract.
(b) Annual projected build-up of cash value in insurance contract.
(c) Available cash in the event of death of the insured (death benefit).
(d) Annual outlay savings.
(e) Annual outlay borrowing.
* Major national insurance company illustration (policy provides 18 year guarantee at illustrated premium).

FIGURE 5H

6 How to Use Trusts in Estate Planning

Many people understand the concept of a will but not the concept of a trust. A major distinction is that a will manages assets only after death. A trust, on the other hand, can provide for the management of assets during life.

Modern estate planning and trusts go hand in hand. As we learned in Chapter 4, wills usually distribute only part of our estate assets. We can create trusts to receive, manage, and distribute all that we own. In this chapter we will explore both basic trusts and several specific trusts that are used in estate planning.

■ WHAT IS A TRUST?

In simple terms, a trust is an entity created to own assets. The assets can be of various types—cash, stocks, bonds, real estate, business interests, collections, and almost any other sort of tangible assets.

> *Trust*—a legal entity that can own assets.

There are typically three parties to the trust:

- The grantor is the person who sets up the trust, names the beneficiary and the trustee, and transfers the assets to the trust.
- The beneficiary is the person or institution named to receive the benefits of the trust.
- The trustee is the person or institution named to manage the trust.

> *Grantor*—the person who sets up the trust, names the beneficiary and the trustee, and transfers the assets to the trust.
>
> *Beneficiary*—the person or institution named to receive the benefits of the trust.
>
> *Trustee*—the person or institution named to manage the trust.

Figure 6a shows the basic dynamics of a trust.

Let's now define trusts more completely. A trust is a formal written agreement by which a person (the grantor) enables a person or an institution (the trustee) to hold and manage assets for the benefit of a person or an institution (the beneficiary) in accordance with the instructions in the trust agreement.

In explaining the dynamics of a trust, we've kept the three parties in the singular—grantor, trustee, beneficiary. But a grantor can name more than one trustee and/or more than one beneficiary.

In setting up the will, the grantor provides written instructions for the

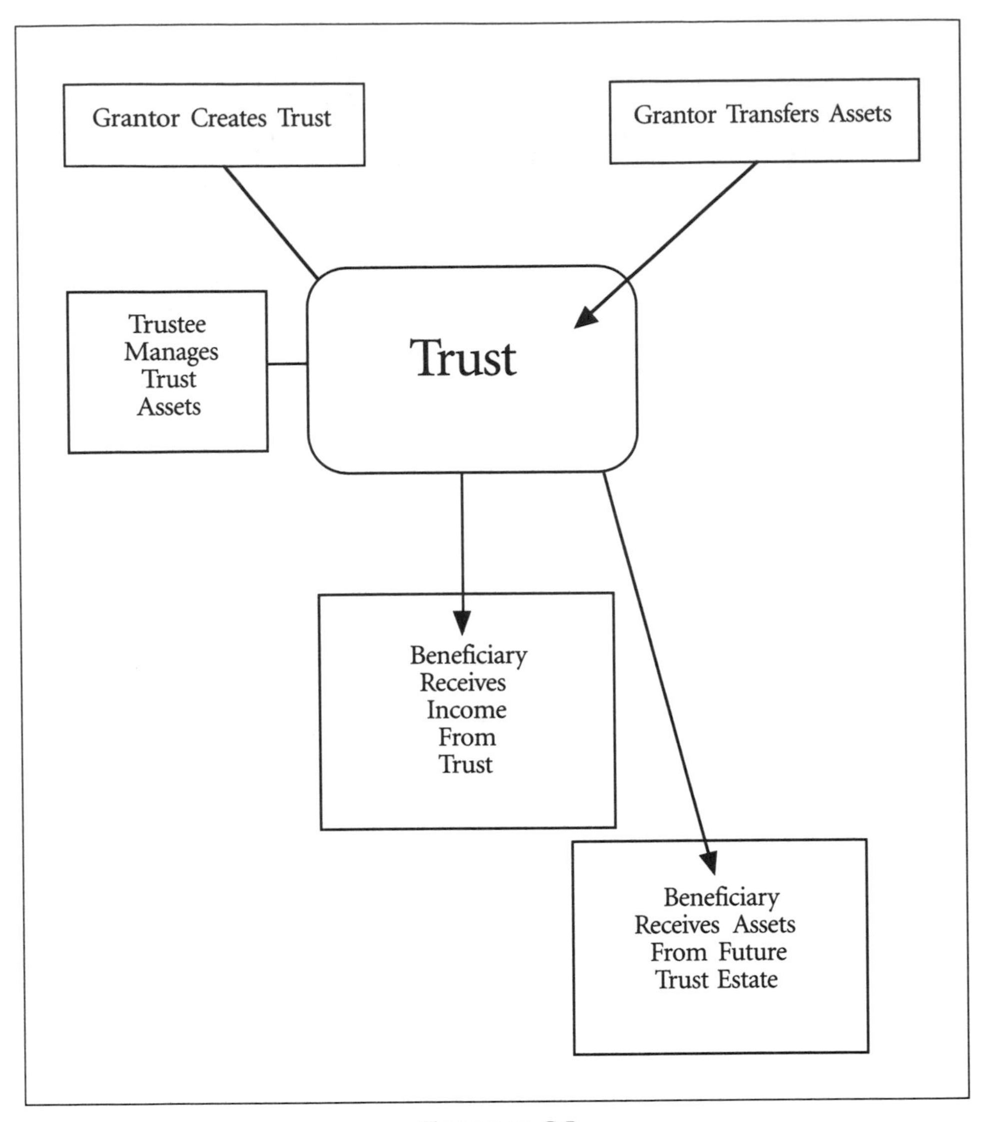

FIGURE 6A

trustee concerning how he or she is to manage or distribute the trust assets. These instructions can be quite basic or very specific.

Trusts can be fairly simple or very intricate, depending on the purposes and the circumstances. But the basic trust dynamics remain constant.

■ TYPES OF TRUSTS

There are two main types of trusts—*living* trusts and *testamentary* trusts.

A *living* trust is any trust that you create during your lifetime. A living trust is also called the inter vivos trust (a Latin term meaning "between or among the living"). This type of trust can be funded (assets transferred to the trust) or not funded (left empty until later), depending on what the trust is meant to do. (We'll later discuss how empty trusts are used.)

> ***Living trust***—any trust that you create during your lifetime. Also called an inter vivos trust.

A *testamentary* trust is created by your will. It really isn't a trust at all until after death. Then the provisions that are written into the will allow for the type of trust to be set up and specify how it is to be funded.

> ***Testamentary trust***—any trust that you create through your will.

The distinction between living wills and testamentary wills is basically a matter of life and death. That seems like a very important difference, doesn't it? But many types of trusts can be created as either living trusts or testamentary trusts—with some differences. So, here at least, the difference between life and death can be of little importance.

Far more important in practical terms are the distinctions among the various types of trusts in terms of what they do and how they work. In this chapter we'll discuss the types of trusts that will be most useful to you in estate planning.

Basic Living Trust

Think about the three players in the trust game—the grantor, the beneficiary, and the trustee. In a basic living trust, the grantor can play all three roles. (That would be impossible, of course, in a testamentary trust!)

A person can set up a trust that he or she manages as trustee and/or from which he or she receives all the benefits as beneficiary. Since nobody lives forever, the grantor also names a second trustee and a second beneficiary. This trustee and this beneficiary are called *contingent* because they assume those roles only when the grantor dies.

> ***Contingent beneficiary***—person named to succeed the grantor of a living will who has named himself or herself as beneficiary.
>
> ***Contingent trustee***—person named to succeed the grantor of a living will who has named himself or herself as trustee.

Upon the death of the grantor, the contingent trustee steps in to manage or distribute assets and the contingent beneficiary begins to receive the assets from the trust. In a simple living trust, that may happen immediately.

However, the grantor may have left trust instructions for the trustee to hold assets for a period of time before distributing any or all of them. This would be the case, for example, if the grantor named minor children as contingent beneficiaries of the trust.

The transfer of legal roles from the grantor as trustee and beneficiary to the contingent trustee and the contingent beneficiary happens without probate involvement. In fact, many living trusts are set up for the sole purpose of keeping estate assets from going through probate.

But death is not the only contingency for which you can plan by naming a contingent trustee. What if you become disabled or incapacitated? Who would manage your assets?

The living trust allows you to plan for such an unfortunate event. If you place those assets in a living trust and provide for the possibility of disability or incapacitation, your contingent trustee can take over the management of the trust assets without any involvement of the court system.

(We'll take a more detailed look at planning for incapacity in Chapter 10.)If you want to control how your assets are handled while you're alive or after your death, you can do so with a living trust. The flexibility of the living trust is restricted only by your imagination and goals. There are some legal restrictions, of course. You should use a qualified attorney to draft the trust document.

A word of caution about living trusts: a trust can manage only assets that it owns! A very common mistake is to have an attorney draft a living trust and then not title assets to the trust or to purchase new assets and forget to title them to the trust. If you want a trust to manage assets, the trust must own those assets.

Pour-Over Will

A document that typically accompanies a living trust is the *pour-over will.* This is a will that directs property to go to another legal entity, usually a trust.The process is simple: you set up a living trust and then include a provision in your will that names your trust as beneficiary of the residuary estate—something like "I bequeath my residuary estate to The J.J. Jones Trust." Then, upon your death, the executor of your will takes care of your specific bequests and pays death taxes and claims against the estate, then pours over the rest of the estate into the trust.

Pour-over wills do not avoid probate. They simply direct the distribution of some probate estate assets into a living trust.

> ***Pour-over will***—a will or a provision in a will that directs property to go to another legal entity, usually a trust.

Credit Shelter Trust

The credit shelter trust provides a way to use the unified credits of both husband and wife and to generate income for the surviving spouse. (This trust is known under various names—credit shelter family trust, family trust, bypass trust, B trust, family credit shelter trust, credit trust, and exemption trust.)

The credit shelter trust is perhaps the most common type of trust used in estate planning. It has numerous variations.

It is customarily designed to receive the maximum amount ($650,000 in 1999) that can pass free of federal estate tax upon the death of the first of two spouses to die. The grantor has complete control over where the trust assets are ultimately distributed. The terms of the trust frequently provide for all of its income to be payable to the surviving spouse for life. It can also distribute principal if the terms so

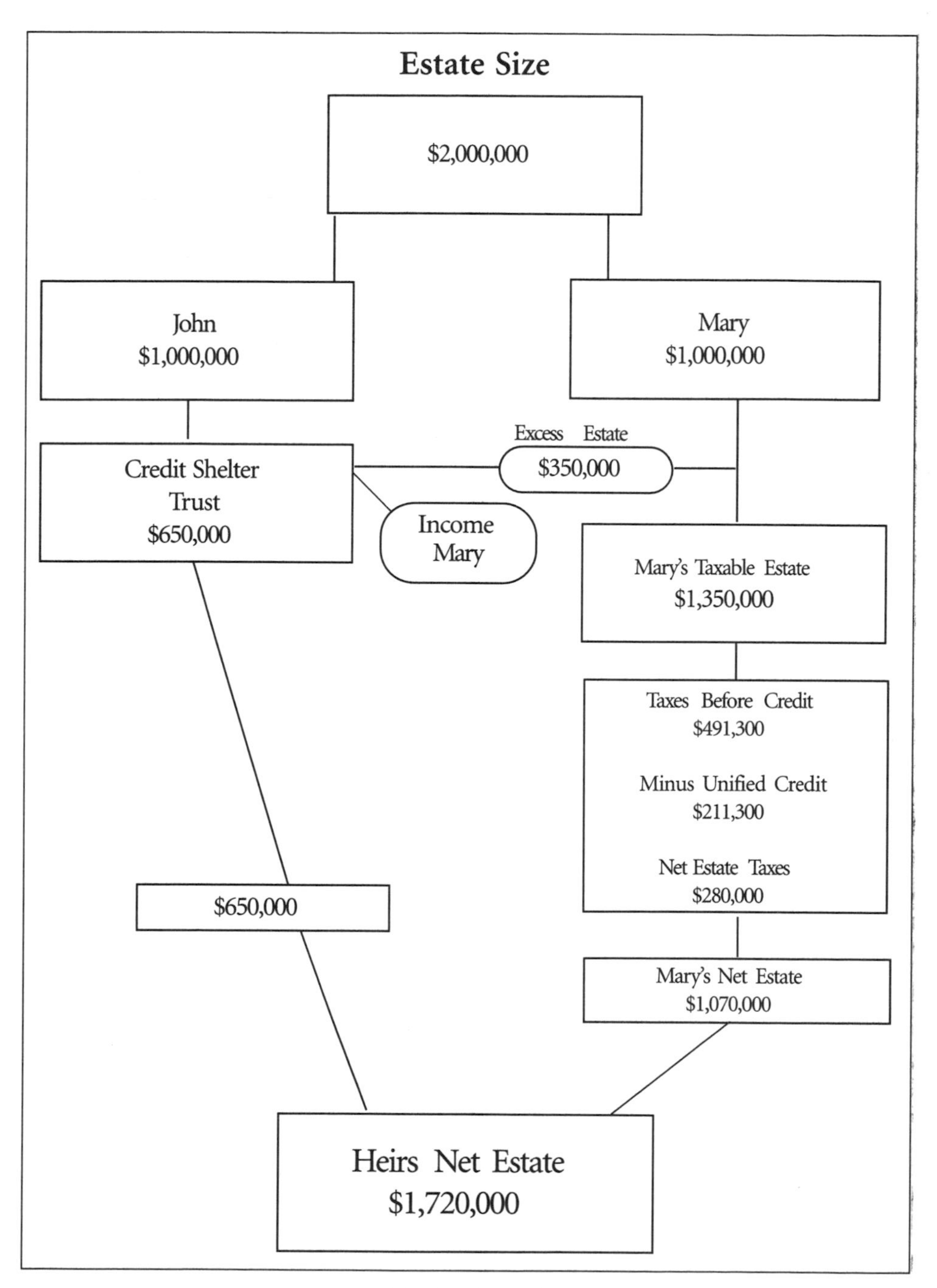
Estate Size
$2,000,000
John
$1,000,000
Mary
$1,000,000
Credit Shelter
Trust
$650,000
Excess Estate
$350,000
Income
Mary
Mary's Taxable Estate
$1,350,000
Taxes Before Credit
$491,300
Minus Unified Credit
$211,300
Net Estate Taxes
$280,000
$650,000
Mary's Net Estate
$1,070,000
Heirs Net Estate
$1,720,000

FIGURE 6B

indicate and certain criteria are met. Then, when the second spouse dies, the assets pass directly or through a trust for one or more beneficiaries, according to the instructions of the first spouse, bypassing the estate tax.

> ***Credit shelter trust***—a trust that reduces estate taxes by using the unified credits of both husband and wife and generates income for the surviving spouse. Also known as credit shelter family trust, family trust, bypass trust, B trust, family credit shelter trust, credit trust, and exemption trust.

> **Note:** a grantor can fund a credit shelter trust only with assets that he or she owns separately. So if you and your spouse own everything jointly, you'll need to retitle the assets that you want to place in the trust.

Qualified Terminal Interest Property (QTIP) Trust

A common type of trust used in estate planning is the qualified terminal (or terminable) interest property (QTIP) trust. The QTIP trust is often a testamentary trust, set up for the benefit of a spouse.

As we saw in Chapter 3, Figure 3d, an effective way for a married couple to minimize estate tax is by using the unified credit exemption for both husband and wife. However, one of the problems in that example was that Mary didn't receive any income from John's estate.

The QTIP trust takes advantage of the unlimited marital deduction, so when it receives assets, it defers potential estate taxes. It also provides income for the surviving spouse.

A QTIP trust must meet two criteria:

1. It must distribute trust income to the surviving spouse during his or her lifetime. (It can also distribute principal if the terms of the trust so indicate and if certain criteria are met.)
2. It must be subject to estate taxes when the surviving spouse dies. The assets are then distributed according to the instructions of the first spouse.

None of the principal of the trust may pass to anyone other than the spouse during his or her lifetime. At the second spouse's death, the assets in the QTIP Trust are included in calculating the estate tax on the second spouse's estate. What remains after paying any estate taxes is distributed in accordance with the provisions of the trust as established by the grantor.

> ***Qualified terminal (or terminable) interest property (QTIP) trust***—A trust that takes advantage of the marital deduction, provides income for the surviving spouse for life, and allows the grantor to determine to whom the trust assets will pass when the surviving spouse dies.

It's very important to recognize that the reason why these estate tax savings strategies work is that both John's and

Mary's estates were properly funded. They each had an estate large enough to take advantage of their unified credit personal estate exemption.

When creating hypothetical examples, this is very easy to do. In the real world, the types of assets that make up an estate and how they are titled will have a great impact on how well an estate plan will work. Balancing estate assets between husband and wife can be very challenging. Meticulously maintaining the proper balance of estates and titling allowing for proper distribution will determine the effectiveness of your estate plan.

In our example in Figure 6c, John's and Mary's estates used both of their unified credit/estate exemptions ($211,300/$650,000 in 1999). Mary receives the income from both trusts and there is no estate tax erosion of assets until she dies. The impact of the estate tax under this combination is essentially the same as in Figure 4b, but John determined the distribution of

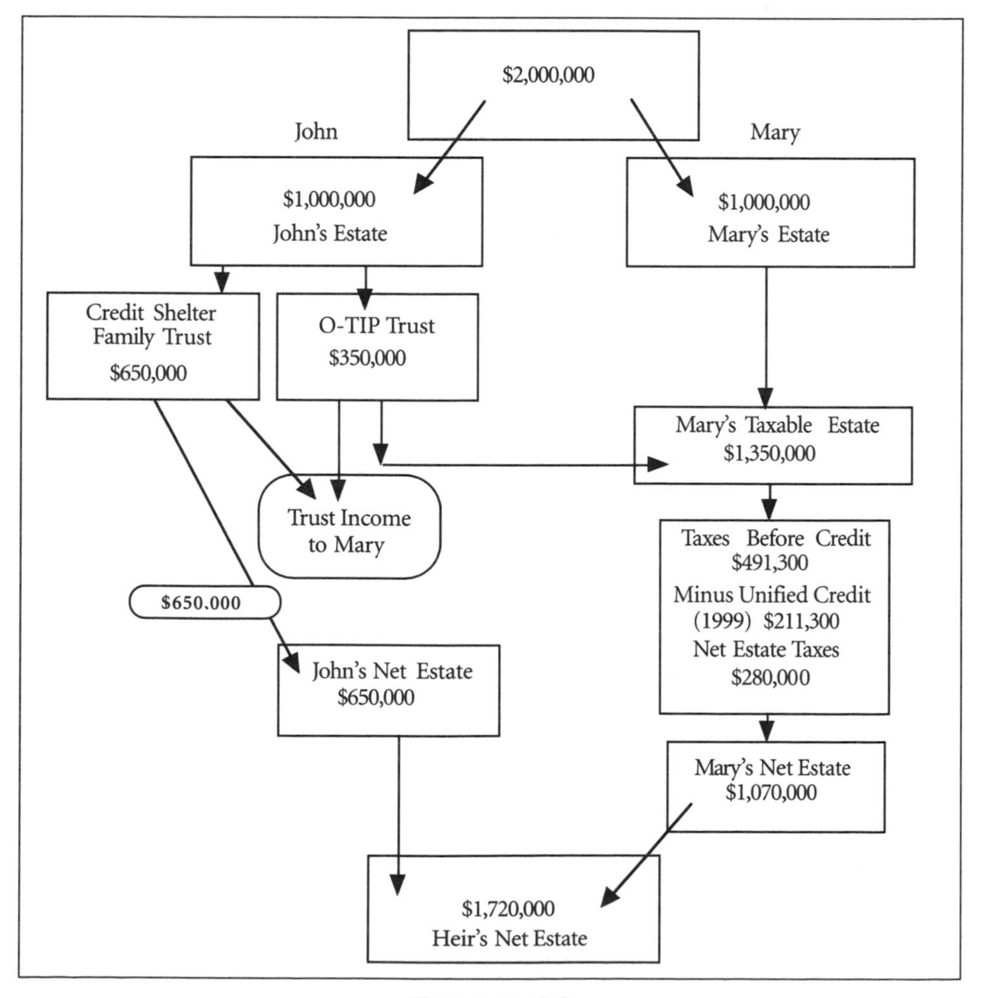

FIGURE 6C

his entire estate, by setting up the QTIP trusts and the credit shelter trust. (See Figure 6c.)

As we noted earlier, this trust goes under various names. But it's still just a trust that works as part of an estate plan to use the unified credits of both husband and wife and minimize the impact of estate taxes.

Qualified Domestic Trust

Most people don't know about the qualified domestic trust. In fact, there's no reason for many people to care about it. In fact, if you and your spouse are both citizens of the United States, skip ahead to the next section.

The Qualified Domestic Trust (QDOT) is a special form of QTIP trust for a spouse who is not a U.S. citizen. Under federal estate tax law, transfers of property to a spouse who is not a U.S. citizen do not qualify for the marital deduction unless they are in this form of trust.

The QDOT keeps any spouse who is not a citizen from receiving assets from a citizen spouse free of estate taxes and then taking the assets back to his or her home country where they will never be subject to U.S. estate tax. Uncle Sam simply wants to make sure that he collects estate taxes from everybody.

A Comment About Life Insurance

There are many good reasons for life insurance, whatever your age. Life insurance can provide immediate cash or an income stream for your family. And, as we showed in Chapter 5, life insurance can also provide liquidity to pay estate taxes and/or to fund a business buy/sell arrangement.

Yet there's a point that many people misunderstand about estate planning: although a life insurance death benefit is not subject to income tax, it's included in your taxable estate if you own the policy. This point is so often missed that it can hardly be overstated.

Let's take the situation of John and Mary as an example. Assume that John owns a $500,000 life insurance policy on himself. This death benefit would increase the size of his estate to $1,500,000. Let's take a look at the impact that the benefit would have on their combination of credit shelter trust and QTIP trust in their estate planning. (See Figure 6d.)

The estate tax jumped by $222,000—44.4% of the $500,000 death benefit! In other words, Uncle Sam collected almost half of the life insurance proceeds—even though he was not named on the policy as a beneficiary! The eventual net death benefit from the insurance policy for the heir was only $278,000.

That's because, if you own a life insurance policy, the proceeds are included in your estate when determining estate taxes, although they're not subject to probate proceedings unless you name your estate as the beneficiary. Although a life insurance policy can be an excellent idea, the proceeds can substantially increase the value of your estate and the amount of estate taxes that must be paid at some point.

Irrevocable Life Insurance Trust (ILIT)

There's a way to prevent Uncle Sam

from becoming a beneficiary of your life insurance policy. You can set up an irrevocable life insurance trust (ILIT) to own the policy and keep the death benefit proceeds outside your taxable estate. This trust can save a family tens of thousands of dollars in estate taxes.

> ***Irrevocable life insurance trust (ILIT)***—A trust that owns a life insurance policy, so that death benefit proceeds do not enter the estate and get taxed.

The method for paying premiums

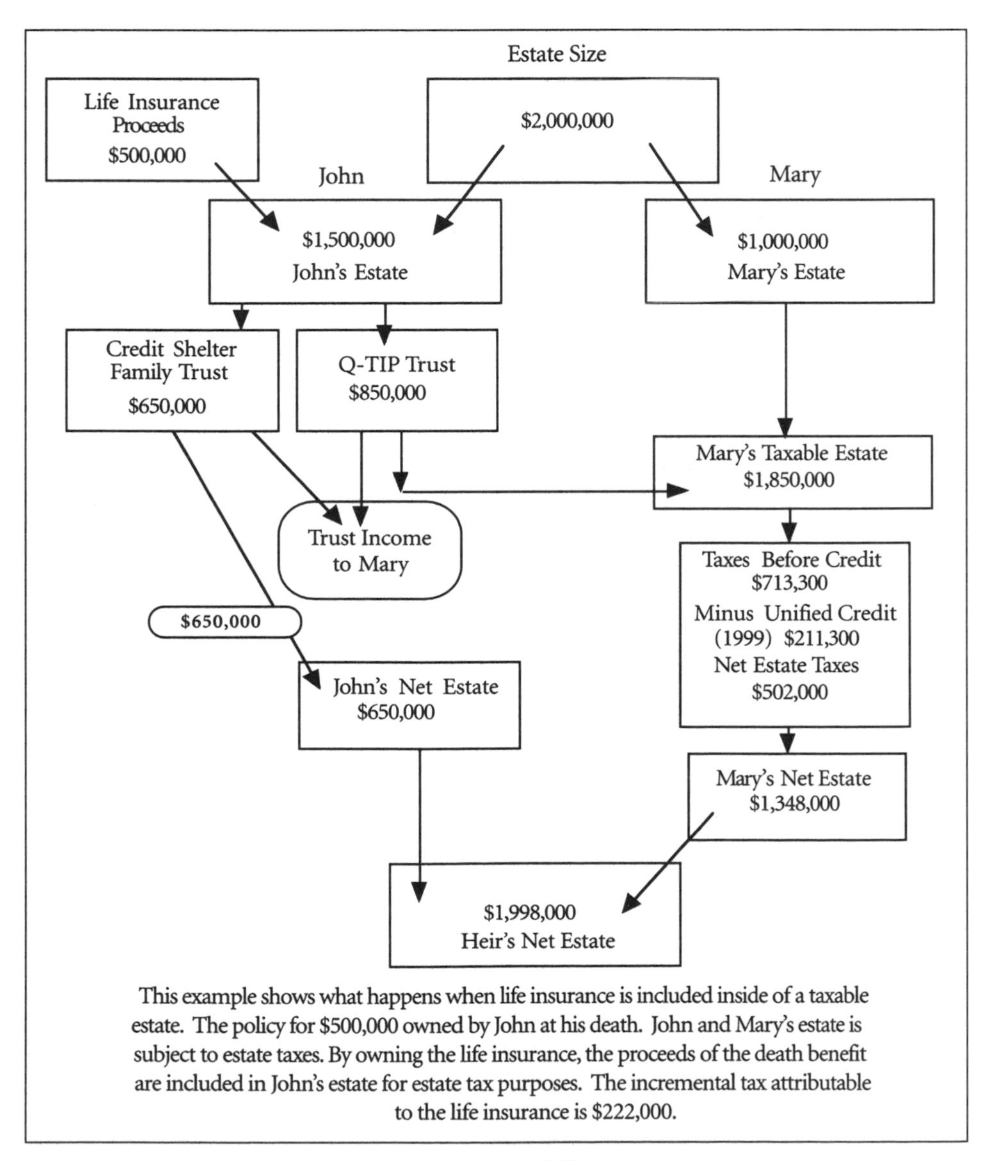

This example shows what happens when life insurance is included inside of a taxable estate. The policy for $500,000 owned by John at his death. John and Mary's estate is subject to estate taxes. By owning the life insurance, the proceeds of the death benefit are included in John's estate for estate tax purposes. The incremental tax attributable to the life insurance is $222,000.

FIGURE 6D

from the ILIT trust is to make gifts to the trust for beneficiaries. Special features of the trust cause these gifts to be "present interest" gifts, which allows the transfers to the trust to be exempt under the $10,000 annual gift rule.

> ***Present interest gift***—a gift that the recipient has the right to use immediately.

Figure 6e shows how John and Mary can set up an ILIT and name their heir as beneficiary, so that the life insurance proceeds pass directly to the heir. That way, their heir benefits from the entire $500,000 in death proceeds without any increase in estate tax liability.

You can easily understand from our example how an ILIT, by protecting life insurance proceeds against estate taxes,

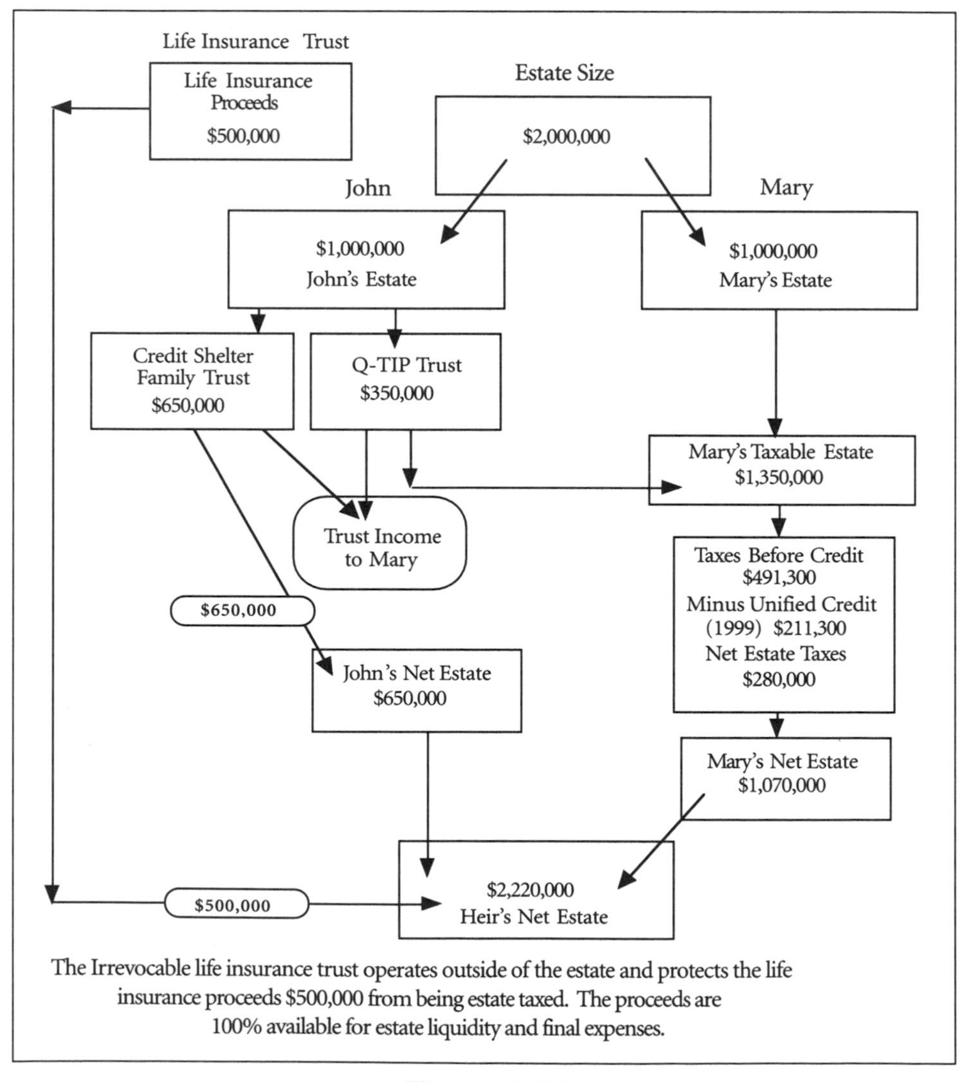

The Irrevocable life insurance trust operates outside of the estate and protects the life insurance proceeds $500,000 from being estate taxed. The proceeds are 100% available for estate liquidity and final expenses.

FIGURE 6E

can be a powerful tool in estate planning. A life insurance policy owned by an ILIT can provide instant liquidity and eliminate estate shrinkage caused by estate taxes and other final expenses.

We offer you three pieces of advice here.

First, don't wait to title your life insurance policy in an ILIT or you might get caught by the three-year rule. What's that? Well, if a person dies and has owned what the legal folks call "incidents of ownership" in a life insurance policy during the last three years of his or her life, the proceeds are included in that person's gross estate. This rule is intended to prevent terminally ill individuals from avoiding estate tax on insurance benefits by transferring ownership of a policy immediately prior to death. So, if you want to take advantage of an ILIT, don't delay.

> ***Incidents of ownership***—all or any control over a life insurance policy, including the rights to borrow against the policy or change the beneficiary.

Second, keep in mind that transferring ownership of life insurance to an irrevocable trust may result in a gift tax. The gift value is the total of premiums you've paid so far or the current cash value of the policy, depending on the type of policy. If the value is $10,000 or less, this transfer can come in under the annual limit for gifts.

Third, since the ILIT is an irrevocable trust, you give up all of your ownership rights. That means that you cannot borrow against your policy or change your beneficiaries.

Now you know the advantages and the disadvantages. You may want to consult an estate planner. For a single person with an estate of more than $650,000 (1999) including life insurance or a married couple with an estate over $1,300,000, an irrevocable life insurance trust may be appropriate.

■ GENERATION-SKIPPING TRANSFER TAX

Historically, wealthy families have used trusts and other techniques to pass property down through several generations without paying estate tax. How does this work?

Here's an example. A man creates a trust and names his son and his grandchildren as beneficiaries—his son to receive income from the trust during his life and then his grandchildren to receive the assets held in the trust. The advantage of this planning would be that it provides some financial benefit from the trust assets to one generation without incurring any estate tax upon the transfer to the next generation. Because the son in our example has no right to the trust assets, when he dies the assets are not included in his taxable estate.

This is what's known as a generation-skipping transfer, because the assets in the trust go from the grantor to his grandchildren, skipping his son. The trust that allows this transfer is called, as you might expect, a generation-skipping trust.

> ***Generation-skipping transfer***—The passing of assets from the owner to his or her grandchildren, so that they are never in the

possession of the owner's child or children.

Generation-skipping trust—A trust that allows assets to bypass a generation, so that grandchildren receive property directly from their grandparents, without it passing through their parents.

We began this section with an important word—"historically." That's because generation-skipping trusts are largely a thing of the past.

Why use a generation-skipping trust? To avoid estate taxes. So, how does Uncle Sam feel when people find legal ways to avoid paying taxes? He creates more laws.

The law created in this case (passed in 1976, then repealed, and finally re-enacted in 1986) imposes a separate estate tax structure known as the generation-skipping transfer (GST) tax. The GST tax is intended to complement the federal estate tax by restricting taxpayers from transferring wealth to successive generations free of estate taxes. So, very wealthy families can no longer use generation-skipping trusts to keep very big estates from a very big tax bite. But there's still a little relief possible through generation-skipping trusts, as we'll explain shortly.

The GST Tax is applied to:

- Direct skips
- Taxable distributions
- Taxable terminations

OK. What does that mean in English?

If you make a transfer directly to a descendent who is more than one generation below you (your grandchildren or great-grandchildren or beyond), the GST Tax will apply. That's known as a *direct skip.*

If you create a trust for a child and name grandchildren as secondary beneficiaries, any distributions made from the trust to the grandchildren will be subject to the GST Tax, one way or the other. If the trust distributions to the grandchildren come while their parent is alive, they're called *taxable distributions.* If the trust distributions to the grandchildren come when the trust terminates, they're called *taxable terminations.*

Now you understand how the generation-skipping transfer tax works. So, what's the bottom line?

The GST tax is substantial—the tax rate is 55%, the highest estate and gift tax rate. Ouch!

But the generation-skipping trust is not completely a thing of the past. It remains alive, to some extent at least, through the generation-skipping tax exemption.

Every individual is allowed a GST tax exemption of $1,000,000. (As part of the Taxpayer Relief Act of 1997, this amount will be indexed for inflation, but will increase only in $10,000 increments.) This exemption may be allocated to property or assets that a person transfers while alive or when he or she dies. A married couple may combine the two exemptions and transfer up to $2,000,000 without paying the GST tax.

The very wealthy can no longer avoid hefty estate taxes by using generation-skipping trusts. But if you have a large estate, you should certainly consider using your GST tax exemption.

■ A TRUST THAT IS NOT A TRUST

Since the focus of this chapter is trusts, we should include here a few words about something that's called a trust but is not technically a trust—the Totten trust.

What is called a Totten trust is actually a bank account that the owner titles in such a way that, upon his or her death, the contents pass to one or more other named beneficiaries without going through probate.

> *Totten trust*—A shared bank account that belongs to the depositor until he or she dies, then passes to the designated beneficiary. Also known as a payable-on-death (or pay-on-death) or POD account, informal trust, or bank trust account.

Once you sort through all the various names, this "trust" is actually very simple to understand and use.

You open a bank account in your name, as depositor and as "trustee for the benefit of __beneficiary__." The person whom you designate as beneficiary will assume ownership of the account when you die. However, as long as you live, the beneficiary has no rights to the account. You can do with it as you like—even spend all the money in the account. Upon your death, the beneficiary simply presents the bank with proof of his or her identity and a certified copy of your death certificate.

If you'd like to designate more than one beneficiary, the process is the same, except that after you name the beneficiaries, you add the wording "equal beneficiaries." That way, your beneficiaries will each enjoy an equal share of the account.

It's as simple as that. Well, in principle. If the beneficiary dies before the depositor and there's no successor beneficiary named, the money in the account transfers as part of the residuary estate, according to the terms of the will for the distribution of the residuary estate.

The benefit of a Totten trust is that the money in the account bypasses probate. However, the account is included in the taxable estate of the depositor.

Although this "trust" is usually set up as a new account, you can also add a trust designation to a current account. Totten trust accounts are usually savings accounts or certificates of deposit accounts, but they can be checking accounts as well.

It's easy to open a Totten trust. Most banks and credit unions have standard forms and can handle the paperwork for you.

7 Getting More Out of Giving: Charities and Your Estate

Charity means giving from your heart. Now we're going to show you how you can also give from your head. In this chapter we'll try to cover some of the basics and provide enough information to highlight the benefits of charitable giving in estate planning.

Many people give to charities, regularly or at least occasionally. They give to religious organizations, educational institutions, hospitals, local and national charities, and foundations. The contributions that charities receive from generous donors help keep them operating. In fact, without that generosity many charities would cease to operate.

But how many people with good intentions would give even more if they knew how? There are ways to give from the heart and from the head. That's where estate planning can help all of us help our favorite charities—and get more out of giving.

■ WILL

Probably the most common way to benefit charities—and reduce your taxable estate–is to make a charitable bequest through your will. Any gift bequeathed to an approved charity is exempt from federal and almost all state gift and estate taxes. That tax advantage provides a little extra incentive to give.

But which charitable causes should you support with a bequest? Maybe you already have some favorites. If not, then we recommend that you contact the following agency:

National Charities
Information Bureau
19 Union Square West
New York NY 10003-1997
Phone: (212) 929-6300
Fax: (212) 463-7083
Web: http://www.give.org

The NCIB publishes a quarterly, *Wise Giving Guide*, which includes a Quick Reference Guide that lists close to 400 national organizations. The guide can help you make a more informed decision about donating.

It's relatively easy to name a charity as a beneficiary of your will. Many charities, especially churches, conduct seminars to explain how to do just that. But there are two points that we'll mention here because they're important and can avoid problems for your estate.

The first point is to make sure that whatever charitable cause you choose qualifies as tax-exempt. Normally, this means that the organization has tax-exempt status under Section 501(c)(3) of the Internal Revenue Code. This status should be stated somewhere on any materials provided by the organization. If you're not sure about an organization you're considering, contact the IRS to check whether it's on the list. (That's not an easy task. According to Independent Sector, in 1996 there were 654,000 501(c)(3) organizations!)

Note: The IRS has installed an electronic version of Publication 78, "Cumulative List of Organizations," on its World Wide Web site http://www.irs.ustreas.gov/prod/bus_info/eo/eosearch.html. You just enter the name and city and state of an organization and you get a brief statement about it, including the percentage of the deductibility limitation.)

The second point is to have a backup plan. It's not likely to happen, but what if an organization you name as beneficiary loses its tax-exempt status or just ceases to exist? In the former case, your bequest will still go to the organization, but you'll lose any tax advantages. In the latter case, your bequest will probably end up in your residuary estate.

That's where it's wise to have a backup organization. You simply name a second beneficiary, just as you would for any other beneficiary of your will, as we explained in Chapter 4.

■ PLANNING FOR LEVERAGE

Contributing to charities through a will is a very good strategy. But it has no impact on your financial position during your lifetime. Yet many people would like to do more while they're alive—particularly if they knew how to leverage their dollars for the benefit of the charity.

In many cases, charitable planning shifts money from taxes to charity. (If your favorite charity is Uncle Sam, the next few pages may be of little interest to you.) Planning can allow you to support charitable causes yet maintain or even increase the amount you leave to your heirs. We'll focus here on two basic types of giving: life insurance and charitable remainder trusts.

■ LIFE INSURANCE

A very simple way to leverage a gift to your favorite charity is through life insurance. You just name the charity as the beneficiary and as the owner.

Because life insurance is an investment, it generally pays out significantly more than you pay into it. This appreciation in value makes it an excellent way to leverage your charitable dollar.

When you make a charity the owner and beneficiary of your life insurance policy, you gain two advantages. First, you can deduct the premiums from your income taxes as a charitable contribution. Second, your gift removes the policy proceeds from your taxable estate.

■ TRANSFER OF ASSETS

Pop quiz: Which is worth more, $100,000 in cash or real estate that has appreciated in value from $25,000 to $100,000?

Answer: the property is worth more–at least if you give it away.

Let's take an example. Assume that John is planning his estate and wants to make a charitable contribution of $100,000. John owns a piece of real estate that he purchased for $25,000 and that is now worth $100,000. He plans on selling the property because he does not need it and believes it has peaked in value. John also has a discretionary $100,000 in cash to give to the charity. Which asset should he give?

If John gives the cash, he gets an income tax deduction of $100,000. If John gives the real estate instead, he still gets a $100,000 deduction, but he escapes the capital gains tax that he would have faced if he'd sold the property.

What does John gain in this transaction? He receives a charitable deduction of $100,000 and saves the tax he would have paid on $75,000 of realized capital gain. Assuming that his capital gains tax rate is 20%, he saves $15,000 in tax.

(The benefit to the charity remains the same whether John donates cash or property. So, if you answered the pop quiz with "Neither," you're right–from the perspective of the charity. But John would have another perspective.)

Let's assume now that John wants to benefit the charity but is unwilling to give away $100,000. Also, he wants to sell the real estate and reinvest the net proceeds to receive income, but he's reluctant to sell because of the capital gains tax.

There's a way that John can get what he wants and at the same time benefit the charity. It's called the charitable remainder trust.

■ CHARITABLE REMAINDER TRUST

What's a charitable remainder trust? A CRT is a trust that benefits both you and whichever charity you choose.

How does it work? It's as easy as 1-2-3:

1. You set up a trust with a onetime contribution of principal.
2. You name two types of beneficiary–an income beneficiary (yourself, someone else, or several people) and a final beneficiary (the charity of your choice).
3. You designate a period of time or life.

The trust then pays an annual sum to you or whomever you name as income beneficiaries over a specified period. Then when the income beneficiary dies, the charity named as final beneficiary receives the remainder of the assets in the CRT. (That's why it's called a remainder trust.)

> ***Charitable remainder trust***—A gift made in trust to a qualified charity, an arrangement that regularly pays income from the assets to the donor or another beneficiary during the donor's lifetime and then passes the remaining assets to the designated charity.

That's easy enough, even when we throw in some numbers. The annual payments to the beneficiaries must be at least 5% but no more than 50%. The present value of the amount going to the qualified charity must be at least 10% of the amount contributed. When that specified period ends, the remainder of the principal is transferred to the charity.

(We should remind you that if the income beneficiary is anyone other than you or your spouse and the annual payout is more than $10,000, you'll have to pay a gift tax. So don't be too generous with the payout–or split it among two or more beneficiaries.)

OK. Now let's throw in another detail. The charitable remainder trust is available in two forms: the annuity trust and the unitrust. The difference is slight, but potentially significant:

- The annuity trust pays the income beneficiary a fixed amount each year, no matter what—a steady income stream.
- The unitrust pays a percentage of the value of the trust assets and any accumulated earnings, as evaluated every year. If the unitrust assets appreciate, the payout increases; if the assets lose value, the payout is less.

Whether the CRT is set up as an annuity or as a unitrust, it's a trust that works partly for the benefit of the donor (in most cases) and partly for the benefit of the charity.

Let's take as an example the situation with John and his $100,000 piece of real estate. John transfers the real estate to a charitable remainder trust. The trustee then sells the real estate and reinvests the proceeds of $100,000. There's no capital gains tax because the CRT is a tax-exempt entity. Then, every year John receives income from the trust. If he chooses the minimum 5% payout rate, he receives $5,000—exactly (if it's an annuity) or more or less (if it's a unitrust).

John pays income taxes on the income as he receives it. But he would have paid income tax up front if he'd sold the real estate and reinvested the difference. But if he had sold it, he would have had only $85,000 to invest, which at 5% would have yielded $4250.

Figure 7a shows how John uses the CRT to receive an additional $750 a year, transfer the property for the benefit of the charity, and remove the $100,000 from his estate without incurring a gift tax or using any of his unified credit.

Wealth Replacement Trust

When we discuss transferring an appreciated asset transferred to a charitable remainder trust, people frequently ask, "What about my heirs?" That's a very good question. And we have a very good answer—the wealth replacement trust.

This trust does exactly what the name states: it compensates the heirs for the assets transferred to a charitable cause. The wealth replacement trust is an irrevocable life insurance trust (ILIT) that a person sets up as both owner and beneficiary of a life insurance policy on his or her life, as we discussed in Chapter 6.

> ***Wealth replacement trust***—A trust set up to compensate heirs for a contribution to charity of assets that would otherwise have been included in the estate for the heirs.

The face value of the policy will be the amount the donor wants to leave to the heirs—usually the value of the

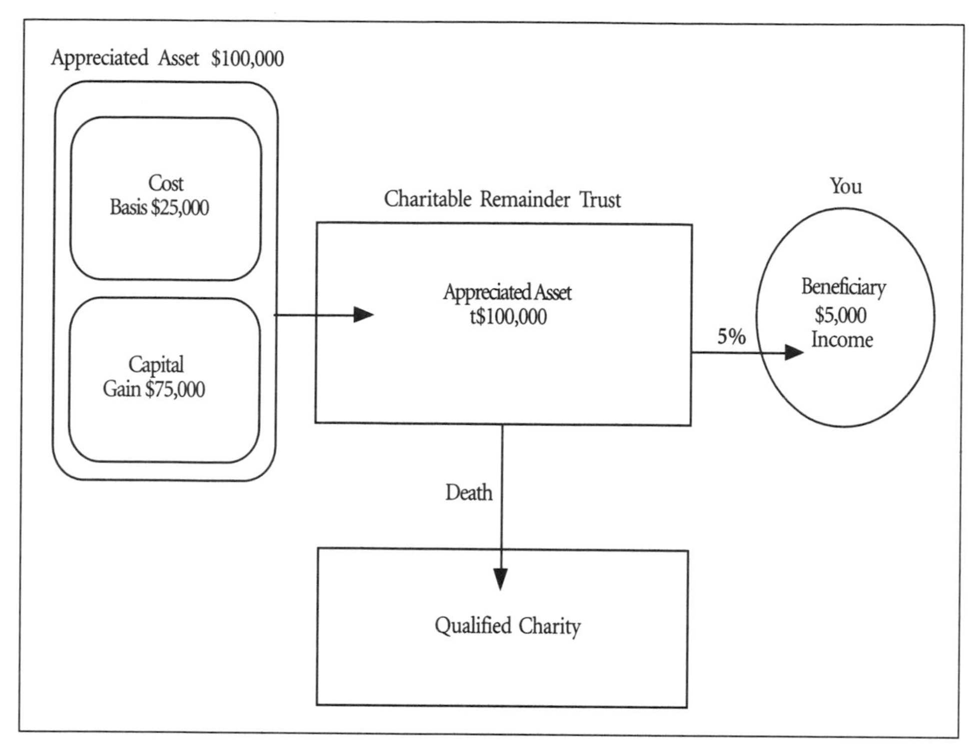

FIGURE 7A

asset given to the charitable remainder trust. The donor pays the premiums on the life insurance policy each year. (One source of funds for paying these premiums may be the savings from the charitable contribution.)

The trustee of the wealth replacement trust (this is often the donor) then pays the premium due on the life insurance policy out of the funds transferred to the trust. This happens every year until the donor dies or pays in full for the policy. Then, when the donor dies, the proceeds from the life insurance policy are distributed to the heirs as beneficiaries of the trust. As we discussed in Chapter 7, the ILIT holds the policy outside the estate, so the proceeds are not subject to estate tax.

Of course, the IRS places a few restrictions on wealth replacement trusts. The tax code requires that the heirs have a present interest in the trust. How can heirs have a "present interest" in a life insurance policy? By having the right to the cash paid for the premiums. So, every year, before gifting the premiums into the trust, the donor must inform the heirs that they have a right to the money and they must then waive this right.

> ***Present interest***—the right to use a gift immediately.

Let's look at the example of John's transfer. Obviously, after he sets up a CRT for his $100,000 property, his estate will be worth $100,000 less to his heirs. If that's a problem, here's a solution for John–and maybe for you, too.

As Figure 7c shows, John transfers $100,000 of appreciated property to a CRT. Then, to replace the "lost" assets in his estate, John purchases a life insurance contract inside an irrevocable life insurance trust. The ILIT holds the policy outside the estate for estate tax purposes and John has an additional $750 annually that he can use to pay the insurance premiums. When John dies, the assets in the charitable remainder trust pass to the charity and the $100,000 death benefit from the life insurance inside his wealth replacement trust passes to his heirs without estate tax.

The significance of this becomes clear when we analyze the combined savings in capital gains tax, income tax, and estate tax. First, John saved approximately $21,000 in capital gains taxes by transferring the real estate to the CRT. Second, he receives a charitable income tax deduction in the year in

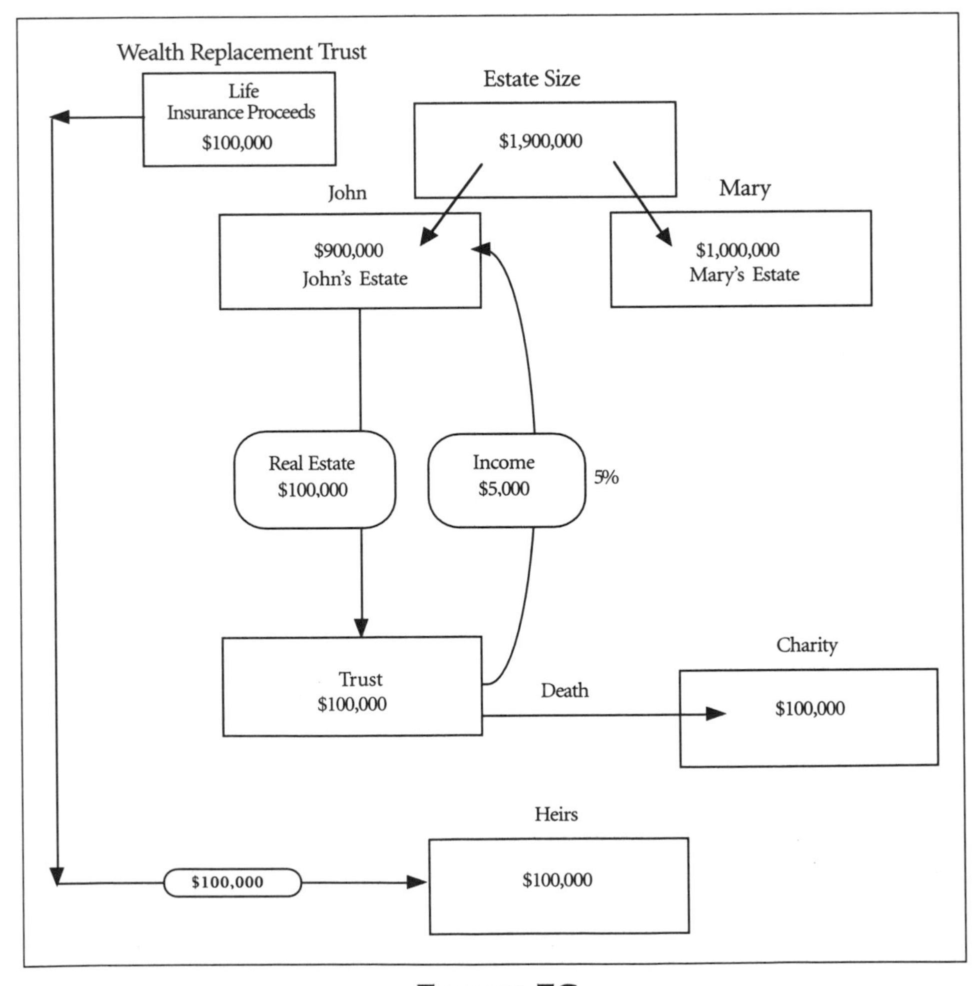

FIGURE 7C

which he places the property in the trust. (The amount depends on his age.) Third, exclusion of the real estate from his taxable estate saved $39,000 in estate taxes.

The bottom line: John saves at least $60,000 in taxes. By using excess earnings to help pay premiums on the $100,000 of life insurance, John replaces the asset to his heirs at no cost.

That's a creative way to use a CRT. Here's another, which can solve a common problem in taxable estates–retirement plans.

Retirement plan distributions are subject to income tax and the assets remaining in the plan at death are subject to estate tax. If the account is substantial, that can cause a problem.

So how do you avoid those taxes? You set up a charitable remainder trust as the beneficiary for your retirement plan and name your spouse as income beneficiary of the CRT.

As we see in Figure 7d, John has $200,000 in a qualified retirement plan. He names as beneficiary a charitable remainder trust. This strategy allows him to avoid paying any taxes on the distribution from the plan and removes the $200,000 from his taxable estate. He sets up the CRT to pay income to Mary and then, when she dies, the $200,000 in the trust passes to the designated charity.

Here's the result. There are no income or estate taxes payable at death, because qualified charities don't pay

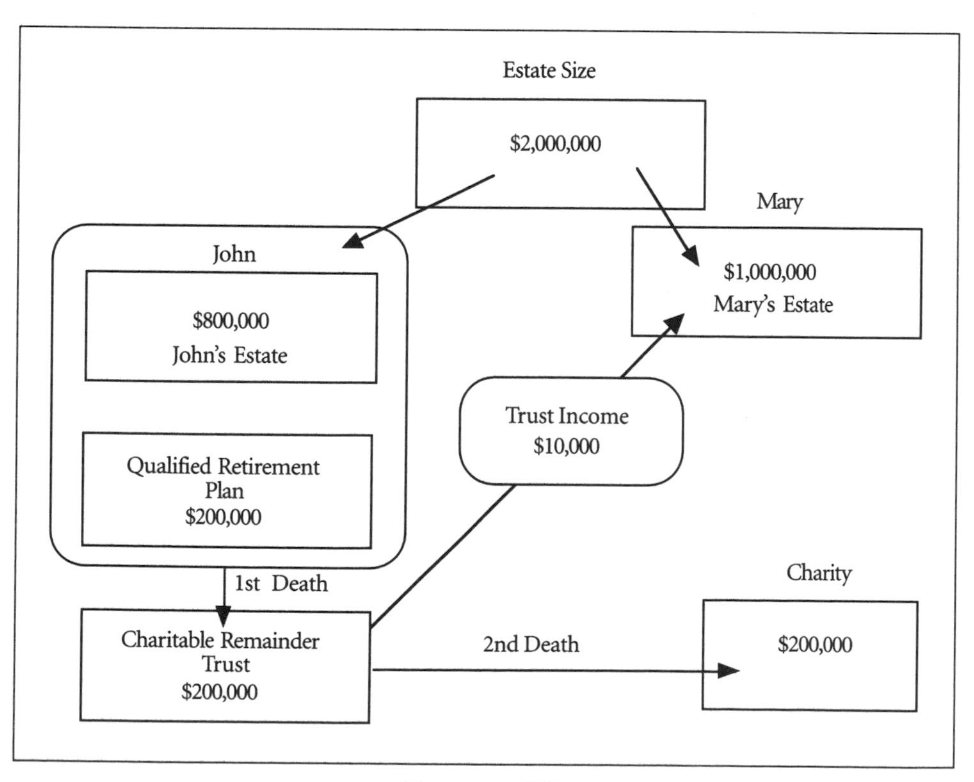

FIGURE 7D

income or estate taxes! The retirement plan is removed from your taxable estate. Your spouse pays income tax on the distributions that are made, but if he or she doesn't need the income, it can be used to fund a wealth replacement trust for the children.

> **Note:** If you want to use this strategy for taking care of a qualified retirement plan, you'll need special legal documents. We recommend that you consult a tax attorney to handle this matter properly.

Leaving your qualified plan assets to a specific charity or to a charitable remainder trust will save estate and income tax. By giving your qualified plan assets to charity, you create a 100% charitable deduction for estate and income tax purposes. If you use a CRT, the charitable deduction is based on the present value of the remainder interest left to charity.

You can transfer assets to a charity either during your life or at death. In both cases, the assets are removed from your estate without using any of your unified credit on the transfer. Generally, a transfer to a charity or a charitable remainder trust does not create an income tax or estate tax liability. It does not act as a trigger for capital gains on appreciated assets and it may even create an income tax deduction.

So, give until it feels good, emotionally and financially.

8 Planning for Your Retirement

Retirement. That one word can evoke so many pleasant images and ideas for most people. Of course, we're not all going to agree on what would make us happy, but we certainly can agree that we should enjoy all those years after we punch out for the last time.

And we certainly can take some actions now that will help ensure that we can get the most out of our golden years. And, to a great extent, the degree of gold that we enjoy will depend on the amount of green and silver that we own.

Developing a plan to ensure financial independence is increasingly important, yet it's also increasingly complex. The realities of retirement are changing. Consider the following facts:

> "Medical science is increasing life expectancies by 15 to 20 years."
>
> "Truth About Retirement," *Fortune*, Dec. 25, 1995

> "Responsibility for retirement funding is shifting more and more from businesses to individuals."
>
> *USA Today*, May 8, 1995

> "About one in four pension plans has promised more benefits than it can pay with current reserves."
>
> "The Windfall," *Profiles*, March 1994

> "75% of the wealth in the U.S. is in the hands of the people age 55 and older. Experts estimate that $1 trillion in assets will transfer to the next generation in 10 years."
>
> "Betting on the Boomers," *Fortune*, Dec. 25, 1994

The bottom line is that you need to take care of your money so your money can take care of you.

There are a variety of financial strategies and products that seniors can use to help outpace inflation, minimize taxation, and preserve their estates.

■ HOW MUCH WILL I NEED?

"How much income or assets will I need to have a comfortable retirement?"

For every person who asks this vital question, there are at least a handful of answers, depending on circumstances and perspectives. So let's try to sort out a few realities here.

Every individual has different and unique needs. A general rule of thumb is that you need 75% of your salary, adjusted for inflation, to retire comfortably. But, as Figure 8a shows, that percentage will vary according to your level of income when you retire: you naturally expect your assets to support you in the style to which you've accustomed yourself.

1996 Estimate Of Retirement Income Need And Social Security Allocation To Income*

Pre-Retirement Income (a)	Percent Needed In Retirement (b)
$20,000	76%
$30,000	72%
$40,000	71%
$50,000	74%
$60,000	74%
$70,000	77%
$80,000	84%
$90,000	86%
$150,000	86%
$200,000	87%
$250,000	89%

Key:

(a) Level of pre-retirement income.

(b) Percent of pre-retirement income needed in retirement.

* Source: Georgia State University for Risk Management

FIGURE 8A

And that style will likely change. Maybe you just want to sit in a rocking chair. Well, after you buy that rocker, you won't need much else. But maybe that's not your style. Maybe you intend to travel around. Maybe you want to buy a second home. If that's your style of retirement, if that's what you mean by "retire comfortably," then you'll be incurring a few extra expenses.

We suggest that you take an hour or so to just sit back, dream about retirement, and make a list of the things that you'd like to do. Then start jotting down some figures, putting price tags on your dreams. Don't forget to include the basics, such as food, clothing, utilities, transportation, and so forth. Even if your vision of retirement is a tropical island, you'll still need some cash from time to time!

Then, once you've got a better idea of how much you'll need, we can move on to the next question.

■ HOW MUCH WILL I HAVE?

This is a question that only you can answer. But we can cover a few generalities and help you think about that question and come up with a better answer.

When you ask people about retirement income, many will immediately mention Social Security. Well, that's a start. So let's check out some figures.

■ SOCIAL SECURITY: WHAT WILL YOU GET?

You can check Social Security records of your earnings and get a statement of your estimated benefits. Call your local Social Security office or 800-772-1213 and ask for the Request for Personal Earnings and Benefit Estimate Statement, Form SSA-7004. Four to six weeks later, you'll receive a statement of earnings as reported by your employer(s). If you think the record is wrong, contact your local Social Security Administration office. You can use W-2 tax report forms or pay stubs to support your claim.

When can you start collecting full Social Security benefits? Somewhere between ages 65 and 67, depending on when you were born (Figure 8b).

You can collect a reduced benefit if you retire at age 62. But unless you need the money, it's better to leave it in your account. If you work beyond the full retirement age and keep on contributing, you increase your benefits. If

1996 Social Security Table of Age To Receive Full Social Security Benefits

Year Of Birth	Full Retirement Age (years)	Additional Months
1937 or earlier	65	0
1938	65	2
1939	65	4
1940	65	6
1941	65	8
1942	65	10
1943 to 1954	66	0
1955	66	2
1956	66	4
1957	66	6
1958	66	8
1959	66	10
1960 and later	67	0

*Source: Social Security Administration.

FIGURE 8B

you die before your spouse, he or she will be entitled to your benefits; the exact amount will depend on your spouse's age.

Two Problems with Social Security

OK. So you know how much you'll get from Social Security and you know when you can start tapping that resource. But there are two problems to consider.

First, the usual problem—taxes. Your Social Security benefits will be taxed if your income is higher than the base amount set by Social Security. You'll owe federal and state income taxes on up to half your benefit amount if your AGI plus your tax-exempt interest plus one-half your Social Security benefit is more than $32,000.

Second, too much money. That's not usually a problem, of course. But if you're collecting Social Security benefits and earning money, you may be penalized, depending on your age and the amount of money you earn. The rules change every January 1. For 1999 the rules are as follows:

- Over age 70: no limit on earnings.
- Ages 65-70: no more than $15,500. For every $3 you earn over the limit, your payment is reduced by $1.
- Ages 62-65: no more than $9,600. For every $2 you earn over the limit, your payment is reduced by $1.

(Contact your local Social Security office for more information.)

So, now we've covered the big question for you—What will I get? And we've answered a few little questions associated with collecting those benefits.

Now we should comment on that other question about Social Security—How long will the system last?

In 1940, when the first Social Security check was issued, a 65-year-old male could expect to live another 12 years, while a 65-year-old woman could expect another 13 years. Life expectancies have risen: now at age 65 men can expect to live another 15 years and women another 19 years. By 2020 those figures will have risen to 16.5 years and 20 years, respectively.

The average worker retiring in 1996 at age 65 will have paid $21,502 into the system, while his or her employers will have matched that amount, for a total of $43,004. With the average life expectancy, the average man will collect $150,000 and the average woman will collect almost $200,000. As people live longer and collect far more from the Social Security system than they put into it, changes will need to be made to keep the system from collapsing.

So, we can't expect the system to last indefinitely. And even if it continues to endure, we can't count entirely on Social Security to meet our needs in retirement.

Some estimates show that Social Security will provide 60% of the retirement needs for minimum wage earners, but only 28% for those who have earned the maximum Social Security wage or more. So the higher your salary over time, the less Social

Security will figure in your retirement planning (Figure 8c).

This chart conveys a depressing reality. Most of us are not really counting on Social Security to take care of us—but many people are surprised at how little Social Security will contribute to their idea of a comfortable retirement.

So, what percentage of your needs does this chart tell you to meet through sources other than Social Security? And how are you going to do that?

Retirement Plans

Maybe you have a retirement plan, like many people. You may be in a traditional company pension plan, a profit-sharing plan, or a 401(k) plan or equivalent. You can count on that source to cover some or a lot of your needs.

But you've got to take care of that asset or you could lose a little to Uncle Sam. (We love our Uncle, but we don't want to share any more of our retirement comfort with him than necessary!)

1996 Estimate Of Retirement Income Need And Social Security Allocation To Income*

Pre-Retirement Income (a)	Percent Needed In Retirement (b)	Percent Replaced By Soc. Security (c)	Percent Needed From Savings (d)
$20,000	76%	64%	12%
$30,000	72%	55%	17%
$40,000	71%	44%	27%
$50,000	74%	37%	37%
$60,000	74%	31%	43%
$70,000	77%	27%	50%
$80,000	84%	23%	61%
$90,000	86%	21%	65%
$150,000	86%	13%	73%
$200,000	87%	9%	78%
$250,000	89%	8%	81%

Key:

(a) Level of pre-retirement income.

(b) Percent of pre-retirement income needed in retirement.

(c) Percent of pre-retirement income replaced by Social Security in retirement.

(d) Percent of pre-retirement income needed from other resources in retirement.

* Source: Georgia State University for Risk Management

Figure 8c

When you leave the company, you'll probably be able to take the money in your retirement plan either as a lump sum distribution or as an annuity–periodic payments for a specified period of time or for life.

If you take your retirement money as an annuity, consider this. Most retirement plan payouts are not indexed or adjusted for inflation; if the cost of living goes up, the purchasing power of your retirement income will go down. In addition (or rather, in subtraction), if your retirement plan is integrated, the amount of your payout is reduced by the amount of Social Security you receive when you retire.

If you take your retirement money as a lump sum distribution, you have a choice: you can either pay taxes on it or roll the funds over into an individual retirement account (IRA).

If you choose the rollover, make sure to do it through a direct transfer to the new IRA account. If you take possession of the funds for even five minutes, 20% will be withheld as tax. You'll get a full refund–but only if you put the entire amount into the new IRA rollover account within 60 days and file an income tax return. This means that you have to come up with the 20% withheld out of your pocket to complete the rollover.

If you don't roll over the retirement funds within 60 days, you'll have to pay taxes on that money. Also, if you're under age 59 1/2, an additional 10% penalty will be assessed.

(Do you plan on finding another job with a retirement plan? If so, then you'll want to segregate your rollover money in a separate IRA. Don't contribute any money to that IRA from other sources. If you keep your retirement rollover funds pure, you can later roll over that money into the new company retirement plan. Again, do it through direct transfer.)

Tax Deductions

Many people who invest in an IRA can deduct the contribution on their tax return. A $2,000 deduction is available for anyone who is not covered by employer plans or whose adjusted gross income (AGI) is under $25,000 if single or $40,000 if married.

The Tax Relief Act of 1997 set higher AGI limits for deductibility, as we noted in Chapter 2. Figure 8d shows the income maximum for full deductibility and the level past which people no longer qualify for even a partial deduction.

The Tax Relief Act of 1997 has brought other, substantial changes to IRAs.

Any person who does not participate in an employment-based retirement plan is now eligible to make deductible IRA contributions, even if that person's spouse participates in an employment-based retirement plan. (Before 1998, both spouses had to meet the non-participation rule.) Eligibility for this special active participant relief phases out for AGI between $150,000 to $160,000 for joint returns.

There are additional exceptions to the 10% penalty tax for early withdrawal. The exceptions to the 10% penalty tax now include:

- After age 59 1/2

Limits For Deductibility Of Individual Retirement Accounts

Year	Joint Returns (AGI) (a)	Joint Returns (AGI) (b)	Individual Returns (AGI) (a)	Individual Returns (AGI) (b)
1999	$51,000	$61,000	$31,000	$41,000
2000	$52,000	$62,000	$32,000	$42,000
2001	$53,000	$63,000	$33,000	$43,000
2002	$54,000	$64,000	$34,000	$44,000
2003	$60,000	$70,000	$40,000	$50,000
2004	$65,000	$75,000	$45,000	$55,000
2005	$70,000	$80,000	$50,000	$60,000
2006	$75,000	$85,000	$50,000	$60,000
2007	$80,000	$100,000	$50,000	$60,000

Key:
(a) IRA fully deductible up to this amount.
(b) IRA partially prorata deductible up to this amount. Non-deductible if over this amount.

* Source: Internal Revenue Service

FIGURE 8D

- On or after death or disability
- As part of a series of substantial equal periodic payments made for life or life expectancy
- First home purchases (up to $10,000)
- Higher education expenses for the IRA account holder, and his or her spouse, child, or grandchild

Roth IRA

The Tax Relief Act of 1997 created a new type of individual retirement account, the Roth IRA, as we explained in Chapter 2. This IRA is funded with after-tax dollars. The contributions and earnings can be withdrawn income tax free if the IRA is at least five years old and the owner is 59 1/2 or older at the time of distributions.

Income tax-free distributions typically have been reserved for tax-free municipal bonds. This move by Congress will create huge opportunities to enjoy tax-free growth and distribution of returns. The Roth IRA has another incredible feature: unlike the traditional IRA, it has no minimum distribution requirements after age 70 1/2. A person can grow the IRA tax-free in the investment vehicle of his or her choice. This is unprecedented in the world of income taxes!

Conversions

Many investors are likely to decide that they will be better off making contributions to a Roth IRA rather than the traditional IRA. But it may be tougher deciding whether it pays to convert IRA assets into the new account.

IRA investors with an AGI of less than $100,000 can convert all or part of the money in their IRA accounts into the new Roth IRA. Future earnings in the Roth IRA can be withdrawn tax-free after age 59 1/2 if the account has been in place for at least five years. However, the investor must pay income taxes on the taxable portion (earnings plus deductible contributions) of the amount converted to the Roth IRA. The 10% premature withdrawal penalty does not apply to conversions.

So, if you have a traditional IRA, you face a decision. Should you pay some taxes now and withdraw future earnings tax-free (assuming you'll hold the account at least five years)? Or should you leave the money in your current IRA, where it will continue to grow tax-deferred, and then pay taxes on all earnings and deductible contributions upon withdrawal?

Some of the factors to consider in making this decision include:

- How much time you have until you begin taking the money out
- How long you expect to be making withdrawals after retirement
- The rate of return you expect to earn on your savings before and during retirement
- The total amount you might convert, since you would have to pay taxes on the taxable portion of it
- Your current tax bracket and the tax bracket you project for your retirement years

Generally, the more time you have before you start taking the money out and the higher the rate of return you expect, the more advantageous it may be to convert the money into the Roth IRA. That's because the more you accumulate in earnings, the more valuable the advantage of withdrawing those earnings free of taxation.

If you're close to retirement, it may not be as worthwhile to make the conversion. Also, the larger the amount you convert, the more cash you will need to pay the taxes. It's not worthwhile to do a conversion if you plan on taking money out of the assets in your IRA to pay the taxes due. However, if you pay the taxes from other assets, you should definitely consider conversion.

If you don't want to be required to withdraw your money, the Roth is the way to go. The Roth IRA has no mandatory withdrawal age or minimum distribution requirements. You can keep your money in a Roth IRA indefinitely or leave it for your heirs, who would receive the holdings free from federal income taxes.

All IRA contributions before 1987 were made with pre-tax dollars. Since 1987, nondeductible contributions have also been allowed. Taxes are owed only on the earnings for those contributions. If you've made nondeductible contributions, you must have a record to establish the portion of your distribution that's not subject to income tax. Nondeductible contributions in the future should be made to the Roth IRA.

SIMPLIFIED EMPLOYEE PENSION

Another type of retirement plan similar to the IRA is the Simplified Employee Pension (SEP). An SEP Plan is a pension plan designed for small business owners and self-employed individuals. It's a simple, inexpensive alternative to the more complex and expensive qualified retirement plans such as 401(k), profit sharing, and pension plans.

> ***Simplified Employee Pension (SEP)***—A simple, inexpensive pension plan designed for small business owners and self-employed individuals as an alternative to the 401(k), profit sharing, and pension plans.

The SEP-IRA is very easy to set up. There are two simple steps:

1. The employer completes IRS Form 5305 or 5305A, normally a single page with a few blanks to fill in. This form establishes the SEP and spells out the plan and participant requirements.
2. The employees must each establish a traditional IRA in order to receive the SEP contributions made by the employer. This IRA has been named the SEP-IRA, but it's just a traditional IRA.

Contributions to the plan are tax-deductible and the earnings are tax-deferred. Contributions are a fixed percentage of your earned net income up to $30,000 maximum annually. SEPs are more flexible and require less reporting than Keogh Plans (an earlier type of plan for small businesses).

ANNUITIES

An annuity is a type of retirement account with a life insurance company. You can put the money into the account in one of two ways: as a lump sum payment or a series of contributions to the account. The money then generates earnings tax-deferred. You can get the money out of the account in one of two ways: as a lump sum or as an annuity stream of income in the future, often after retirement. Either way, the earnings are subject to income taxes, although not the contributions.

> ***Annuity***—investment that pays a fixed amount to a designated beneficiary for a specified number of years or for life.

There are no limits on how much you can invest in an annuity. However, you still must be at least 59 1/2 to withdraw the money without a 10% early withdrawal penalty.

If you convert an annuity to a lifetime income stream (annuitize), you can get regular monthly payments for life or a specific period of years.

Annuities seem to come in pairs. There are two ways to put money into the account. There are two ways to get money out of the account. And there are, generally, two types of annuities–fixed or variable.

Fixed annuities have a guaranteed value and they earn a set rate of interest during a specified period. The rate usually changes once a year.

Variable annuities are very similar to mutual funds. You may choose how the money is invested and you can divide an account among various investments. This could include accounts that invest in stocks, bonds, or combinations.

Which type of annuity is better for you? The advantage of the variable annuity is the opportunity to invest money in investments that have the potential for greater return (although they also have the potential for less return or even loss of principal). The advantage of the fixed annuity is that the principal amount of the account value is guaranteed by the issuing company.

Medicare and Medicaid: What You Need to Know

"Medicare pays for only skilled nursing home care, and 98% of nursing home care is not skilled."

95 Health Benefit Planning Guide for Seniors

"A year in a nursing home will cost from $30,000 to more than 100,000, depending on the area of the country."

Financial Planning, January 1996

"Based on just an average long-term care stay of 2.5 years, the cost to you could be from $75,000 to $250,000."

Long Term Care, Noble Continuing Ed., 1995

"Home Health Care agencies charge $15 to $20 an hour for the minimum level of custodial care. Just 20 hours of custodial care per week cost $400. Skilled care may run as high as $100 per day."

Business Week, April 15, 1996

"Assisted living monthly fees can range from $900 to $3,000 a month."

Provider, October 1995

"Four out of 10 people age 65 or older risk entering a nursing home."

Health Insurance Underwriter, February 1995

"The national average cost for nursing homes is approximately $105.00 per day. Assisted living ranges anywhere from $50—$90 per day. Depending on where you live, you could easily spend $40,000 to $80,000 for a year's stay in a nursing home."

LTC Planner

"Two-thirds of elderly nursing home patients rely on Medicaid to pay for their care. With nursing home costs averaging $40,000 a year, about half of residents who begin by paying with their own money and health insurance must turn to Medicaid within three to five years."

"Bill to Protect Nursing Home Residents Goes to President," Associated Press, March 15, 1999, HealthCentral.com (http://www.healthcentral.com/News/)

"How much does a nursing home cost? Plenty. As a national average, a year in a nursing home now costs between $25,000 and $30,000, and in some places as much as $50,000."

AV Limited Publications (http://www.avlimited.com/nursing/nursing.htm)

> "There are currently over one million residents in the more than 19,000 nursing homes in the United States. The nursing home population has been growing and continues to grow with the increase in the number of elderly. While only 5% of the elderly population is in a nursing home at any one time, approximately 20% to 30% of all people can expect to spend some time in a nursing home setting."
>
> Seniors-Site.com

> "Generally, older people pay more for long-term care than for anything else they buy. The annual cost of a nursing home stay is approximately $50,000. Home care can also be very costly. An older person who receives just three home health visits per week could pay about $12,000 for home care each year."
>
> "Paying for Long-Term Care," American Association of Retired Persons

Those facts should make all of us think a lot—and maybe worry a little. Our purpose in this chapter is to provide information and help you turn your thoughts and worries into planning and taking action.

Medicare and Medicaid (Medical Assistance) procedures vary from state to state. The chart at the end of the chapter provides the basic players and contact information for Iowa, Minnesota, North Dakota, South Dakota, and Wisconsin.

■ MEDICARE

Medicare is a federal health insurance program primarily for people over age 65. When you start receiving Social Security benefits at or after that age, you'll be enrolled in Medicare automatically. You'll receive a Medicare card that shows the coverage to which you're entitled and the date your coverage begins.

> ***Medicare***—federal health insurance program primarily for people over age 65 who are receiving Social Security retirement benefits.

Costs Covered by Medicare

Medicare consists of two parts. Part A is paid for out of Social Security taxes and is free to anyone qualifying for it. Part B is an optional program that carries small monthly premiums.

Medicare Part A, commonly known as Hospital Insurance, is mandatory. It covers medically necessary hospital and related health care. Part A includes costs for such expenses as inpatient hospital care necessitated by acute illness, skilled nursing home care, certified hospice care for the terminally ill, inpatient psychiatric care, and care in the home by a certified home health care provider.

Medicare Part B, commonly known as Supplemental Medical Insurance, is optional health insurance. It's intended to cover some of the costs not covered by Medicare Part A, such as outpatient hospital services, outpatient physical therapy, speech pathology services, necessary ambulance service, and medical equipment.

The federal government contracts with private insurance companies to handle routine claims processing, payment, and other functions under Parts A and B. Private insurance companies contracted under Part A are called fiscal intermediaries. Private insurance companies contracted under Part B are called carriers.

> *Fiscal intermediary*—A private insurance company that contracts with the federal government to provide Medicare Part A coverage.
>
> *Carrier*—A private insurance company that contracts with the federal government to provide Medicare Part B coverage.

If you have any questions about Medicare that we don't cover in this chapter, you can call the national Medicare hotline at 800-638-6833 or the appropriate number listed at the end of this chapter.

Anyone eligible to receive RSI or railroad benefits is eligible for Medicare Part A coverage, although it's not necessary to be receiving money benefits through either of these two programs in order to receive Medicare benefits. Anyone age 65 or older not eligible for RSI or railroad benefits can still receive Medicare Part A coverage by paying a monthly premium. Medicare Part B coverage is automatically available to anyone who qualifies for Medicare Part A benefits. In fact, all applicants for Medicare Part A benefits are automatically enrolled in Medicare Part B unless they opt out of Part B coverage.

If you have any questions, contact the nearest Railroad Retirement Board field office, call 800-808-0772, or visit the RRB Web site at http://www.rrb.gov.

Costs Not Covered by Medicare

Medicare was never intended to provide comprehensive coverage for all medical needs of America's elderly population, but only to supplement private resources. Medicare does not cover many health services, such as the following:

- Custodial care that could reasonably be given by someone without medical training and is generally intended to help the patient with his or her daily living needs, such as help with bathing, walking, or exercising
- Dentures or routine dental care
- Eyeglasses or hearing aids and the examinations to prescribe or fit them
- Nursing home care (except skilled nursing care)
- Prescription drugs
- Routine physical checkups
- Related tests

For more information about Medicare, contact the insurance companies listed for your state in Figure 9a.

Medicare Information by State

Iowa

Medicare A Fiscal Intermediary:
Wellmark, Inc., 712-279-8650
Medicare B Carrier:
Blue Cross/Blue Shield of North Dakota, 515-245-4785 or 800-532-1285
United Health Care (railroad retirement beneficiaries), 800-833-4455

Minnesota

Medicare A Fiscal Intermediary:
Blue Cross and Blue Shield of Minnesota, 612-456-8000 or 651-456-8000
Medicare B Carrier:
United Health Care Insurance Co., 800-352-2762 or 612-884-7171
United Health Care (railroad retirement beneficiaries), 800-833-4455

North Dakota

Medicare A Fiscal Intermediary:
Blue Cross and Blue Shield of North Dakota, 800-444-4606
Medicare B Carrier:
Blue Shield of North Dakota, 800-247-2267, 800-332-6681, or 701-277-2363
United Health Care (railroad retirement beneficiaries), 800-833-4455

South Dakota

Medicare A Fiscal Intermediary:
IASD Health Service Corporation, 515-246-0126
Medicare B Carrier:
Blue Shield of North Dakota, 800-437-4762 or 701-277-2363
United Health Care (railroad retirement beneficiaries), 800-833-4455

Wisconsin

Medicare A Fiscal Intermediary:
Blue Cross and Blue Shield of Wisconsin, 414-224-4954
Medicare B Carrier:
Medicare/WPS, 800-944-0051 or 608-221-3330, 800-828-2837 (TTY/TDD)
United Health Care (railroad retirement beneficiaries), 800-833-4455

FIGURE 9A

Insurance Issues Related to Medicare

Many seniors look for some form of private insurance to supplement Medicare coverage. What are your options?

Some seniors are able to get continuation or conversion coverage from group policies they had at their workplaces. Under these plans, seniors continue to be covered by the policies that covered them while they were working.

Another popular option for seniors is to join a Health Maintenance Organization (HMO). HMO coverage is similar to continuation or conversion coverage, but many HMOs have more complicated rules for people covered by Medicare, so it pays to learn about a particular HMO's policies regarding Medicare benefits before signing up.

Another alternative is private insurance policies intended to cover gaps in Medicare coverage, such as deductibles, co-payments, or procedures not covered by Medicare. These policies are formally known as Medicare supplement insurance and commonly called Medigap policies.

> ***Medigap***—health insurance policies that supplement Medicare coverage.

You need only one Medigap policy—although unscrupulous insurance sales people may try to sell you more. Medigap policies are regulated by federal and state laws. It's a federal offense to sell a policy that duplicates the protection you already have.

If you have questions or concerns about a supplemental insurance policy, the State Health Insurance Advisory Program can help (Figure 9b).

■ MEDICAL ASSISTANCE (MEDICAID)

Medical Assistance is a program that pays the cost of medical care if your income and assets are at or below the limits established to qualify as financially needy. The Medical Assistance

State Health Insurance Advisory Program

Iowa 800-351-4664	**South Dakota** 800-822-8804 605-733-3656 (Pierre) 605-773-3656 (Sioux Falls) 605-342-3494 (Rapid City)
Minnesota 800-333-2433	
North Dakota 800-247-0560 701-328-2977	**Wisconsin** 800-242-1060 608-267-3201

Figure 9B

program will pay part or all of your medical bills. It can also cover medical bills you incurred in the three months before the month you apply.

> ***Medicaid***—a joint federal/state program that provides medical care to the needy; the federal government sets minimum standards that all state Medicaid programs must meet and then each state decides how much its programs will cover.

We hope that you'll never need what you're going to read about Medicaid in the following pages. With appropriate planning, you can reduce your chances of ever needing Medical Assistance. But just in case…

■ OVERVIEW OF BASIC MEDICAL ASSISTANCE PLANNING

The following is an overview of basic Medical Assistance planning, provided by Scott Nelson, Attorney on Medical Assistance. It includes recent changes to and/or interpretations of those regulations. It also covers some established and more recently developed techniques in accelerating qualification for the Medical Assistance program. If you do any Medical Assistance planning or any other aspect of estate planning, you should always seek the advice of professionals (attorneys, accountants, financial planners, and trust officers).

A person who needs Medical Assistance starts the process by contacting his or her county human services agency. After submitting the application, he or she must meet with a financial worker, who will explain the program and may ask for more information and verification regarding the applicant's situation. If the applicant is not found eligible, he or she may apply again at any time.

To qualify for Medical Assistance, the applicant may not have more than $3,000 of non-exempt or countable assets. Once qualified, an MA recipient may not keep more than $64 a month of income for personal needs. (The amount varies by state; this is the figure for Minnesota.)

That seems simple enough, in principle, at least if you're single. But for people who are married, the situation gets complicated very quickly.

As you may know, while a couple resides together, Medical Assistance views the couple as a single MA unit. When MA staff apply the asset test for eligibility, they consider all of the couple's total assets, whether those assets are community or separate property, as being available to both partners. So, neither spouse can qualify for Medical Assistance benefits unless both partners qualify as a unit.

- Institutional Spouse (In Long-Term Facility)

  Only $3,000 in assets.
  Monthly income of $64.

- Healthy Spouse

  $81,960 in assets. Monthly income of $1,357. (Community Spouse's Resource Allowance may be increased by excess shelter allowance.)

Only $3,000 in assets? Only $64 a month?

That's right, but there are a lot of complications. Some assets are counted, while others are exempt or unavailable. There are ways to spend down the countable assets, transfer assets, or make them unavailable. But there are also restrictions on what can be done to reach that $3,000 eligibility level. However, a well-conceived spend-down or asset transfer plan can save most of the family unit's resources.

Understanding medicaid law and working with qualified attorneys and planners at the beginning of the process is the best approach. This will allow a family with excess assets to convert assets to period certain income stream based on the Omnibus Budget Reconciliation Act (OBRA) passed in 1993. Complicated, but necessary to plan if asset preservation is important. The social worker works for the county and will not show you how to preserve assets. In many cases, the social worker doesn't understand what can be done.

For example, a family has $250,000 of cash assets (countable assets). The social worker understands that the sick spouse cannot go on medicaid until the family's exempt assets are at $85,000 or below ($3,000 for the sick spouse and $81,960 for the healthy spouse). So the family believes it must spend down to $85,000 of exempt assets.

A skilled professional in this area would explain to the client that the $165,000 of excess countable assets ($250,000 minus $85,000) could be transferred to the healthy spouse. The healthy spouse would then purchase a qualifying medicaid annuity and turn the annuity into a qualifying OBRA '93 period certain income stream based on his or her age. The asset is now protected and the ill spouse is immediately eligible to qualify for medicaid.

Now let's consider various assets and how MA staff would treat them in terms of the MA regulations and under the Spousal Impoverishment Act, a law passed in 1988 to protect the spouse of an applicant for MA by allowing him or her to keep certain amounts of assets and income.

How Medical Assistance Treats Assets

Medical Assistance requires that the couple list all their assets, regardless of whose name they are in, who earned them, or how long either has owned them, including any assets that were transferred within a specified period. (This period is the last 36 months for transfers to any person other than the spouse or the last 60 months for any transfers to a trust.) MA staff then categorize all those assets as exempt or countable or unavailable.

The stay-at-home spouse is then allowed to keep half of the non-exempt assets. This share is known as the Community Spouse Resource Allowance (CSRA). The CSRA minimum in Minnesota is currently $22,828 and the maximum is $81,960. (The CSRA limits can be raised in certain circumstances.)

The applicant and his or her spouse must then either spend down or make unavailable any assets in excess of the $3,000 exemption and the CSRA. Once they've passed the asset test, Medical Assistance then reviews their income and determines the applicant's share of the cost.

Assets That Don't Count

An MA applicant is allowed to keep the following assets, which are not counted toward the $3,000 maximum:

- Household goods
- Clothing
- Jewelry
- Burial space items such as a grave marker, gravesite, crypt, mausoleum, vault, casket, urn, or other repository
- A burial account (up to $1500)
- Interest in a burial account and burial space items
- A motor vehicle (with some exceptions)

Assets That Count

The following assets are counted toward the $3000 maximum:

- Cash on hand
- Bank accounts
- Stocks, bonds, savings certificates
- Contract for deeds for which you hold the title
- Nonhomestead property
- Burial funds in excess of $1,500
- Extra motor vehicles
- Boats

Income. The institutionalized spouse who receives Medical Assistance is allowed to retain a personal needs allowance of $64 a month, as we've mentioned, and a monthly premium to pay for medical insurance. (The personal needs allowance will increase each January 1 by the same percentage as the Social Security cost of living adjustment). All other income is paid to the nursing home except what is needed to pay health insurance premiums, deductibles, or co-payments. There are some exceptions.

Under the Spousal Impoverishment Act, the stay-at-home spouse is allowed a Minimum Monthly Maintenance Needs Allowance of $1,357, a figure that is adjusted annually for inflation. (Again, the CSRA figure can be increased in certain circumstances.)

If the stay-at-home spouse has less than the needs allowance, Medical Assistance will reduce the confined spouse's share of the cost to bring the stay-at-home spouse's income up to the minimum. If the stay-at-home spouse is not receiving any income from the institutionalized spouse, then the stay-at-home spouse may have unlimited income.

Personal Residence. The personal residence is an exempt asset if the MA applicant intends to return home and can reasonably be expected to do so. If the applicant is single and the personal residence is part of his or her probate estate, the personal residence may be subject to asset recovery by the state. If the applicant is married, his or her home is subject to asset recovery when the spouse dies.

The personal residence is also exempt if it's the residence of any of the following people:

- Spouse
- Child under age 21 or blind or disabled
- Brother or sister who owns equity in the home and lived with the applicant for at least one year just before he or she entered the nursing home
- Child or grandchild who lived with the applicant for at least two years just before he or she entered the nursing home and who provided care that allowed the applicant to stay at home

A home can be transferred in limited cases to a child or a sibling. However, the transfer of real property has income, estate, and gift tax and other legal consequences, so you should have a qualified attorney review and complete the transaction.

Whole Life Insurance. Life insurance with a face amount (death benefit) of $1,500 or more is considered an available asset. Does this mean that life insurance needs to be cancelled to qualify for Medical Assistance? No.

Here's an example: the death benefit is $50,000, the cash value is $20,000, the amount at risk is $30,000. The life insurance may be kept in force in two ways. First, the cash value ($20,000) may be made part of the CSRA. Second, the cash value may be borrowed from the policy and invested in an annuitized annuity (see below) and made an unavailable asset. To keep the policy in force, the spouse or the beneficiaries would need to pay loan interest.

Rental Property. Rental property is an exempt asset if it is the primary business of the applicant or spouse. Net income produced is used either as part of the applicant's share of nursing home costs or to provide income for the stay-at-home spouse. If it's not part of a business, it's a countable asset and can be made exempt or unavailable as part of an expanded CSRA through a waiver or an administrative hearing.

Pensions and IRAs. IRAs and pensions, minus any early withdrawal penalty, are an available asset. Under federal tax law, people who are retired and age 70 1/2 or older must take a minimum distribution from IRAs and pensions. The distribution may become part of the Minimum Monthly Maintenance Needs Allowance. Pension accounts may be considered an unavailable or exempt asset if they are under a monthly distribution plan, but they will be subject to the income rules.

Gifts and Asset Transfers. An applicant for Medical Assistance is allowed to make unlimited transfers to his or her spouse and disabled children. These transfers do not create a period of disqualification and they are not subject to a look-back period. However, as we mentioned earlier, other transfers are subject to a look-back period—36 months for transfers to individuals and 60 months for transfers to trusts. Any transfers that do not meet the test may result in a penalty period.

> ***Look-back period***—A waiting period before a Medicaid application is filed or the applicant enters a nursing home.

There are special rules for giving away property or income. If the applicant and spouse give away less than a total of $500 in a month, there's generally no penalty. If the amount exceeds $500, there may be a penalty period.

Trusts. If an individual, his or her spouse, or anyone acting on the individual's behalf establishes a trust using at least some of the individual's funds, that trust may be considered available in determining eligibility for Medicaid.

No consideration is given to the purpose of the trust, the trustee's discretion in administering the trust, restrictions in the trust, exculpatory clauses, or restrictions on distributions. How a trust is treated depends to some extent on what type of trust it is — for example, whether it is revocable or irrevocable and any specific requirements and conditions.

This is how trusts are treated generally:

- Amounts actually paid to or for the benefit of the individual are treated as income to the individual.
- Amounts that could be paid to or for the benefit of the individual, but are not, are treated as available resources.
- Amounts that could be paid to or for the benefit of the individual, but are paid to someone else, are treated as transfers of assets for less than fair market value.
- Amounts that cannot, in any way, be paid to or for the benefit of the individual are also treated as transfers of assets for less than fair market value when contributed to the trust.
- Trusts established by others are not treated as being available.

In all of the above instances, the trust must provide that the state will receive any funds remaining in the trust when the individual dies, up to the amount of Medicaid benefits paid on behalf of the individual.

Finally, a trust will not be counted as available if the state determines that counting the trust would cause an undue hardship.

Health and Dental Insurance. An applicant for Medical Assistance must tell the county agency about any health or dental insurance policies that he or she has. If the local agency decides that a current policy will save money, MA will pay the premiums.

Otherwise, any health or dental insurance would be unnecessary, since MA covers the following care:

- Physician services
- Home health care
- Most prescriptions
- Dental care
- Hospital and nursing home care
- Medical tests
- Physical therapy
- Eyeglasses
- Hearing aids
- Medical equipment

QUESTIONS?

That's a brief but somber look at Medical Assistance. If you have any questions, call your state Medicaid office as listed in Figure 9c.

■ LONG-TERM CARE INSURANCE

Long-term care insurance (LTCI) provides coverage for chronic illness and long-term disability not covered by Medicaid or Medicare. It generally covers the cost of nursing homes as well as certain agency services such as visiting nurses, home health aides, and respite care. Your age, financial situation, and overall health will determine if this coverage makes sense for you.

> ***Long-term care insurance (LTCI)***—Private insurance to cover the high costs of long-term care (also called custodial care) for people with chronic health conditions and/or physi-

State Medicaid Offices

Iowa
Medicaid Director
Division of Medical Services
Department of Human Services
Hoover State Office Building,
Fifth Floor
Des Moines, IA 50319-0114
Phone: 515-281-8794
Fax: 515-281-7791

Minnesota
Medicaid Director
Minnesota Department of
Human Services
444 Lafayette Road
St. Paul, MN 55155-3852
Phone: 651-282-9921
Fax: 651-297-3230

North Dakota
Medicaid Director
Division of Medical Assistance
Department of Human Services
600 East Boulevard Avenue
Bismarck, ND 58505-0261
Phone: 701-328-3194
Fax: 701-328-1544

South Dakota
Medicaid Director
Department of Social Services
Richard F. Kneip Building
700 Governors Drive
Pierre, SD 57501-2291
Phone: 605-773-3495
Fax: 605-773-4855

Wisconsin
Medicaid Director
Division of Health
Department of Health
and Social Services
1 West Wilson Street, Room 250
Madison, WI 53701
Phone: 608-266-2522
Fax: 608-266-1096

FIGURE 9C

cal disabilities who are unable to care for themselves.

For example, LTCI can help you preserve assets for family members if you don't want to spend down your savings to qualify for Medicaid. You can get individual coverage through most life insurance companies. You may also be able to get group coverage for yourself and possibly your parents through your employer or other associations.

The Health Insurance Portability and Accountability Act of 1996 (HIPPA) encouraged the use of long-term care insurance. It changed tax law for LTCI contracts that meet certain federal standards. In general, HIPPA treats certain qualified long-term care contracts the same as health insurance for tax purposes. The premiums for these contracts are deductible in whole or in part, the benefit payments are excluded from personal income, and the unreimbursed cost of qualified long-term care services are deductible as a medical expense.

As with all insurance, you should carefully check the costs, as well as the type and amount of coverage. There's a free booklet that can help you — The Shopper's Guide to Long-Term Care Insurance. Call the National Association of Insurance Commissioners at 816-374-7259 and request a copy.

If you have any questions about long-term care, you might start by contacting the government agency in your state responsible for dealing with concerns in that area (Figure 9d).

State Agencies Responsible for Long-Term Care

Iowa
State Long-Term Care Ombudsman
Iowa Department of Elder Affairs
Clemens Building
200 10th Street, 3rd Floor
Des Moines, IA 50309-3609
Phone: 515-281-4656
Fax: 515-281-4036

Minnesota
State Long-Term Care Ombudsman
Office of Ombudsman for
Older Minnesotans
444 Lafayette Road—4th Floor
St. Paul, MN 55155-3843
Phone: 612-296-0382
Fax: 612-297-5654

North Dakota
State Long-Term Care Ombudsman
Aging Services Division, DHS
600 South 2nd St., Suite 1C
Bismarck, ND 58504-5729
Phone: 701-328-8915
Fax: 701-328-8989

South Dakota
State Long-Term Care Ombudsman
Office of Adult Services and Aging
700 Governors Drive
Pierre, SD 57501-2291
Phone: 605-773-3656
Fax: 605-773-6834

Wisconsin
State Long-Term Care Ombudsman
Board on Aging and Long-Term Care
214 North Hamilton Street
Madison, WI 53703-2118
Phone: 608-266-8945
Fax: 608-261-6570

FIGURE 9D

10 Planning "Just in Case..."

As you have discovered, just having a will does not mean you have a complete estate plan. A will is activated only when you die. What happens if you become incapacitated and are unable to make decisions and manage your affairs?

It's a disturbing thought. Nobody feels comfortable thinking about living with diminished abilities. But that's what happens to thousands of people. Planning now can substantially eliminate problems, both for you and for your loved ones.

Good estate planning involves more than passing on your assets to those you leave behind when you die. It should also involve taking actions, while you are in good physical and mental health, so that somebody can act on your behalf—to make financial, legal, and medical decisions—if you become incapacitated and are no longer able to make decisions.

> *Incapacitation*—in general, the loss of mental competence, the inability to make decisions.

A good estate plan covers the possibility of incapacitation. Otherwise, it may become unnecessarily difficult on the members of your family to pay bills, manage financial affairs, make investment decisions, and possibly run a business.

If you don't make the appropriate arrangements in advance, your loved ones may be forced to petition the court to appoint a guardian or a conservator. That's a tough process in several ways.

■ CONSERVATORSHIP AND GUARDIANSHIP

If a person becomes incapacitated and incapable of making personal or financial decisions, a court may appoint a conservator or a guardian to manage his or her personal affairs, estate, or both.

Guardianship and conservatorship are closely related concepts that vary according to the laws of each state. Here are the basics.

A guardian is a person or an entity appointed to exercise a certain list of powers, including paying for support, maintenance, and education, paying lawful debts, possessing and managing the estate, collecting debts, and instituting lawsuits on behalf of another person, the ward.

A conservator, also known as a limited guardian, is a person or an entity appointed by the court to exercise some, but not all, of these powers on behalf of another person, known as the conservatee.

> *Guardian*—a person who's legally responsible for managing

the affairs and the care of a minor or a person who's incompetent; in some states a conservator plays a similar but more limited role.

Conservator—a person who's legally responsible for managing the financial affairs of a person who's incompetent, playing a role similar to that of a guardian.

To create a guardianship or a conservatorship, any person can petition a probate court. Usually this person is a family member or close friend who's concerned about the person's competence to manage property or make personal decisions.

The petition must set forth the reasons why a guardianship or conservatorship is needed. The petitioner has the burden of proving the person's incapacity. In making its decision, the court applies a standard of the best interest of the person in question.

Conservatorship and guardianship, for most families, are drastic actions—to be used only as a last resort. Family relationships can be terribly strained when a child alleges that a parent has become incompetent and/or if more than one child wishes to be named conservator or guardian or if no child wants the responsibility.

The court procedure for appointing a guardian or a conservator is expensive and often emotionally trying for loved ones. It's also governed by very restrictive rules. The person appointed will be subject to the jurisdiction of the probate court and be required to make annual reports to the court. It may not be possible, for example, to reduce the size of a taxable estate, which means financial losses.

Many of these problems can be avoided if the person, while still competent, creates a durable power of attorney, a living trust, and/or a living will, let's discuss those three tools.

■ POWER OF ATTORNEY

Now, this is where some people get confused—and this confusion has caused problems when a power of attorney has failed to do what it was intended to do. But it's really not complicated at all.

A power of attorney is a document that a person (the principal) signs in order to give another person (the attorney-in-fact) authority to conduct affairs, make decisions, and carry out tasks. However, there are several variations:

- A general power of attorney grants authority to act on your behalf unconditionally and indefinitely, but the authority ends if you become incapacitated.
- A limited or special power of attorney grants limited authority to accomplish a certain purpose or transaction on your behalf in specific situations or for limited time periods.
- A durable power of attorney grants authority to act on your behalf unconditionally and indefinitely and it remains in effect even if you become incapacitated.

- A springing power of attorney is a variation on the durable power of attorney, but the authority takes effect only if you become incapacitated and then only after the doctors have made the necessary diagnosis.
- A durable power of attorney for financial affairs grants authority to handle your financial affairs only.
- A durable power of attorney for health care grants authority to make health care decisions only. (We'll discuss this one a little later.)

Power of attorney—written authorization for someone else to conduct affairs, make decisions, and carry out tasks on your behalf.

Attorney-in-fact—person to whom you give the authority to conduct affairs, make decisions, and carry out tasks on your behalf through a power of attorney.

Only the springing and durable powers of attorney provide the protection that the principal needs against incapacitation. The difference is that the springing power of attorney takes effect only when the doctors have diagnosed incompetence, a diagnosis that may come some time after the person in question has lost the ability to make sound decisions. This is why a true durable power of attorney may be preferable.

■ MAKING IT DURABLE

A durable power of attorney states that the person whom you authorize to act on your behalf will continue to exercise that authority in the event that you lose the capacity. If a durable power of attorney is properly prepared, the person whom you've designated as your attorney-in-fact will be able to handle all of your financial affairs. It will not be necessary to have a court appoint a guardian or a conservator. There will be no restrictions. There will be no added expense. You'll have somebody you trust to take care of your estate when you most need help.

A durable power of attorney gives your attorney-in-fact the legal right to assume responsibility for your financial world. He or she can write checks from your account, pay your bills, buy or sell investments for you, sell or give away any of your property, file your income taxes, and so forth. As the title "attorney-in-fact" indicates, the person you choose will be acting as your legal representative.

Whom should you designate as your attorney-in-fact? Somebody you trust, of course, and who knows you, understands your financial affairs, and is capable of doing as you would wish.

If you're married, a logical choice might be your spouse—if he or she is willing and able to assume that responsibility—or an adult son or daughter. Don't name two or more people to share that power or there will likely be problems. You should also name an alternate.

What makes a power of attorney durable? The document should contain a sentence such as, "This power of attorney shall not be affected by the subsequent disability or incapacity of the principal."

It's usually not necessary to have an attorney draft the document. Most attorneys don't really have any specialized knowledge in this area. In fact, almost all states have a standard form—including Iowa, Minnesota, North Dakota, South Dakota, and Wisconsin.

Your attorney-in-fact would have the right to make gifts on your behalf. This right would be useful, for example, if you're confined to a nursing home and you want to protect your assets from being used to cover nursing home expenses. Your attorney-in-fact would be able to carry out your wishes by making gifts to family members, as allowed by Medicaid-Medical Assistance rules. Another example: if your estate is large enough to be subject to estate taxes, your attorney-in-fact would be able to make gifts to family members to reduce eventual estate taxes.

If you create a durable power of attorney that authorizes someone to manage your financial affairs, you should put those affairs in writing so that your attorney-in-fact will know all about the nature and extent of them. You probably have most of your affairs in order already, if you've prepared a will recently.

Funded Living Trust

Some people choose to plan for possible incapacitation by using a funded living trust. That approach to estate planning is relatively simple in concept, but it can be somewhat complicated in practice.

> ***Funded living trust***—A trust that a person creates during his or her lifetime to arrange for management of his or her assets.

You set up a trust and transfer title of your assets to the trust, which you will administer as trustee. You name a successor trustee to take over the management of the assets owned by the trust in case you become incapacitated.

But here's where things get complicated. What if you fail to transfer all of your property to the trust? What if you receive income from pensions, Social Security, and other sources? That's when it's valuable to have a durable power of attorney, to take care of all of your assets, current and future, incoming and outgoing.

Your attorney-in-fact can transfer the remaining assets to the trust. The trustee can then manage the assets on your behalf, according to the terms you set out in the trust agreement.

Take a look at your estate plan. Does it include a durable power of attorney and a completely funded trust? If not and you become incapacitated, your family may go through pointless suffering and legal complications to manage your assets.

■ DURABLE POWER OF ATTORNEY FOR HEALTH CARE

A durable power of attorney for health care is a specialized form of power of attorney that authorizes an attorney-in-fact to make health care decisions for a principal who has become incompetent.

Durable powers of attorney for health care are valid in all states. State laws govern the extent of the power exercised by an attorney-in-fact. Many states have adopted statutory forms, which usually list the limitations placed by law on an attorney-in-fact.

A health care power of attorney must be signed by the principal or someone acting on behalf of the principal and it must be witnessed by two persons at least 18 years of age or acknowledged by the principal in front of a notary public.

> **Note:** A durable power of attorney for health care is sometimes called a health-care proxy and the attorney-in-fact is then known as the agent.

Just as a legally competent person can create a power of attorney, he or she can revoke it at any time. The only requirement is the principal be legally competent at the time of the revocation.

For the revocation to be effective, the principal must notify the attorney-in-fact (preferably in writing) that the power of attorney is terminated as of a certain date. In the termination notice, the principal should demand that the attorney-in-fact return any power of attorney assets to the principal by that date. The principal should attach a copy of the written termination to the power of attorney document. If the principal has recorded the power of attorney, the revocation must also be recorded.

Choosing a Health-Care Agent

Choosing an attorney-in-fact for health care or a health-care agent is often the most difficult part of this process. You should choose somebody who knows you well, understands your values and beliefs, and can be a strong advocate who will make your wishes known and respected.

A little later in this chapter we provide a list of a few issues that you should discuss with the person you'd like to name to represent you in your durable power of attorney for health care or health-care proxy.

■ LIVING WILLS

A living will is like a traditional will in only two respects:

- Both wills express your wishes in a formal, written way.
- You must be competent to make either will.

A living will is a document spelling out how much and what kind of medical care the person making the will (the declarant) wants should he or she become terminally ill and incapable of communicating his or her wishes. A person may also designate someone as proxy to make these decisions.

> ***Living will***—a document in which a person specifies the kind and extent of medical care he or she wants in the event that he or she becomes terminally ill and incapable of expressing his or her wishes.

Declarant—a person who makes a living will.

Proxy—a person designated in the living will to make health care decisions for the declarant when he or she can no longer do so.

A common perception about living wills is that they are appropriate only for people who do not want extraordinary measures taken to sustain their life. This perception is incorrect. The treatment choices may range from none at all to every possible means of sustaining life.

You do not need a lawyer to draft a living will, although many people have them drafted at the same time that they are having a traditional will drafted. Many people also seek advice from a doctor or religious advisor before drafting a living will because most people would not be able to describe their wishes specifically without first researching the kinds of medical technology currently available to them.

A living will can be very detailed:

- You can direct that certain treatments be given for specific illnesses.
- You can specify a preference for home, hospital, or hospice treatment.
- You can make known any religious objections to a particular treatment.
- You can identify, in advance, any individuals who are likely to try to interfere with treatment decisions and clarify your wishes with regard to those persons.

The most important point about a living will is that it allows you to make decisions in advance about how much and what kind of health care you want. Since the purpose of a living will is to serve as a guide to those who need to make decisions about your care, the more you detail your wishes the more helpful it will be.

In some states, including Minnesota and Wisconsin, the law allows a living will to express wishes concerning organ donation. You may state whether you wish to donate your organs upon death and specify any limitations or special wishes.

For a living will to be valid, there must be at least two witnesses or one notary public. A living will becomes effective when it's delivered to an appropriate health care professional. You should also give a copy to a family member and any family clergy.

It's important for your doctor to know and understand your wishes. When you give your living will to your doctor, he or she must tell you whether or not he or she will comply with it. A doctor has a right to decline to follow the terms of a living will, within the limits of reasonable medical practice. If that's the decision, he or she must help you find another doctor and must make sure that the new doctor is aware of the living will.

Finally, a living will is revocable. You may revoke your living will totally or partially at any time in any manner, regardless of your physical or mental condition.

For further information about living wills and durable power of attorney for health care, contact your state health department (Figure 10a).

States vary in what they call a living will and a durable power of attorney. These forms are often called "advance directives." (In fact, some states have combined living wills and health care power of attorney into a single advanced directive document.) States also have different requirements for making the documents legal.

You can generally obtain state forms and literature from:

- Your local hospital
- Your local nursing home
- Your state or local office on aging
- Your state's bar association
- Your state's hospital association
- Your state's medical association

You can also get advance directive forms from Choice in Dying, a national nonprofit organization. Choice in Dying provides, for a nominal fee, advance directive forms tailored to each state's legal requirements. It pioneered living wills in 1967 and has distributed more than 10 million advance directives since then. The organization monitors legislative changes nationwide and updates all state documents accordingly.

You can obtain advance directives for $5.00 by calling 800-989-WILL (9455) or download an advance directive package (introduction, instructions, and forms) free from the Choice in Dying Web site: http://www.choices.org/ad.htm

Health Care: Choices, Beliefs, Values, and Feelings

As a health-care consumer, you have rights and choices regarding health care. Because making health care choices may raise some sensitive issues, it's often a difficult subject to discuss.

The purpose of this section is to help you think about what could happen to you and to help you choose the most appropriate care based on your personal needs and beliefs. As a way to

Iowa Department of Health
515-281-5605

Minnesota Department of Health
612-623-5460

North Dakota Department of Health
701-224-2372

South Dakota Department of Health, Division of Health and Medical Services
605-773-3737

Wisconsin Health and Social Services
608-266-1511

Figure 10A

guide you through this process, we've included an explanation of commonly used medical terms and questions to help you reflect on your values.

A national law, the Patient Self-Determination Act, went into effect in December 1991 that set universal standards for informing patients of their legal options for refusing or accepting medical treatment. The bill affects all health-care facilities that accept federal funding—hospitals, health maintenance organizations, home health-care services, nursing homes, and hospices.

The law requires each of these facilities, when admitting a patient, to provide a form explaining the state's law regarding acceptance or refusal of medical treatment and the institution's policy concerning it. The staff must ask if you have a living will or health-care proxy and, if not, to make certain choices about your future treatment, in a declaration to physicians.

> ***Declaration to physicians***—a form of living will, a document that specifies your wishes concerning health care treatment.

This is your choice. You are not required, under any circumstances, to create a living will. In fact it's against the law to require anyone to write a declaration to physicians. But if you choose to create one, it must be respected. If you are unable to participate in decision making, in most cases the physician will consult with your family and then your living will.

It's not necessary to complete the form you receive from the health-care facility, but you must answer the question about artificially administered sustenance. Again, you may state that you want your proxy to make those decisions.

> ***Artificially administered sustenance***—providing special nutritional formulas, fluids, and/or medications through tubes when a person cannot take food or fluids by mouth.

Living wills are interpreted only by a doctor. They do not apply in home emergency situations. Paramedics will provide full emergency care.

Once you have written a declaration to physicians or a living will, review it periodically to make sure it continues to be a current statement of your wishes. If you revise it, it's best to fill out a new declaration to physicians and distribute it to all appropriate persons and institutions.

Explanation of Medical Terms

The following information was excerpted from a handbook on living wills provided by Methodist Hospital, St. Louis Park, MN.

Terminal Condition

This is an incurable or irreversible condition in which any medical treatment will only prolong the dying process.

Vegetative State

This is a state in which a person is unable to talk or think or understand others. This condition can be caused by strokes and other diseases of the brain. It is irreversible except in rare circumstances. A person in this state needs support in all aspects of care.

Life-Sustaining Treatment
This is medical treatment that sustains life but cannot cure or reverse a person's terminal condition.

Cardiopulmonary Resuscitation (CPR)
This is a procedure used to restore breathing and a heartbeat that have stopped. It may or may not work. It often involves applying pressure on the chest to keep blood flowing. It may be necessary to put a tube through the mouth or nose to get air moving to the lungs. It may mean connecting a ventilator, to maintain breathing artificially. It may include drugs or electrical shock to restart the heart. CPR may restore the heartbeat, but it does not reverse the dying process.

Respirator / Ventilator
This is a machine that helps a person breathe or that substitutes for natural breathing when a person is unable to breathe because of illness or injury. Use of a respirator or a ventilator requires insertion of a tube through the nose or mouth or a tracheostomy (a surgical opening in the throat).

Dialysis
This life-sustaining treatment is used when kidneys fail to work properly. Dialysis removes waste products from the blood.

Artificially Administered Sustenance
This means giving special nutritional formulas, fluids, and/or medications through tubes when a person cannot drink and/or eat. Intravenous tubes are sometimes used for short-term administration, but the most common methods are through nasogastric tubes (inserted through the nose into the stomach) and a gastrostomy tube (which requires surgery to place the tube into the stomach). This treatment will sustain life but not reverse the dying process.

Do Not Resuscitate (DNR)
This is a physician's order that, in the event of a sudden cardiac or respiratory arrest, no cardiopulmonary resuscitation (CPR) will be initiated. If a DNR order is written in your chart, you will continue to receive medical and nursing care except for CPR.

Brain Death
In this condition, the entire brain has stopped functioning, so the person is dead according to established medical criteria. Only a respirator keeps the person breathing and the lungs functioning.

Reasonable Medical Practice
This term means practice that meets standards of care established by experience and that provides reasonable expectation of benefit for a particular patient in a particular situation and in accordance with state law and organizational policy.

Topics to Discuss with Your Health Care Agent

Before officially designating a health care agent, you should discuss your beliefs and wishes with him or her. The following questions can help guide your discussion.

Think about how you feel about each question. Then tell your health care agent your feelings and any other wishes or desires that he or she should know in order to carry out the responsibilities involved in having authority for decisions about your health care.

Do you think it's a good idea to sign a legal document (a declaration to physicians) that says what medical treatments you want and do not want when you are dying?

Do you think you would want to have any of the following medical treatments performed on you?

- Cardiopulmonary resuscitation
- Respiration
- Dialysis
- Artificial nutrition
- Artificial hydration

Do you want to donate parts of your body to someone else after you die?

How would you describe your current health status? If you currently have any medical problems, how would you describe them?

Do you have any current medical problems that affect your ability to function? If so, what and how?

How do you feel about your current health status?

If you have a doctor, do you like him or her? Why?

Do you think your doctor should make the final decision about any medical treatment you might need?

How important is it for you to be physically independent and self-sufficient?

If your physical and mental abilities were decreased, would that affect your attitude toward independence and self-sufficiency?

Do you expect that your friends, family, and/or others will support your decisions regarding medical treatment you may need now or in the future?

Where would you prefer to die?

How would you prefer to die? For example, would you like to be physically comfortable, to have family members or friends present?

What is your attitude toward death?

How do you feel about the use of life-sustaining measures:

- If you were terminally ill?
- If you were in a permanent coma?
- If you were suffering from an irreversible chronic illness, such as Alzheimer's disease?

What is your general attitude toward illness, dying, and death?

What is your religious background?

How do your religious beliefs affect your attitude toward serious or terminal illness?

Does your attitude toward death find support in your religion?

How does your faith community, church, or synagogue view the role of prayer or religious sacraments in an illness?

What else do you feel is important for your agent to know?

Inform your health care agent about any changes in your health or in your beliefs or attitudes. How well your health care agent performs depends on how well you have prepared him or her.

■ LIFE TENANCY

We discussed life tenancy in Chapter 4, in the context of setting up a life estate, a type of ownership that avoids probate. As you recall, the way it works is that you transfer property to your children, but you reserve the right to use the property until you die. In legal terms, you are the life tenant and your children are the remaindermen.

We should point out here the following possible adverse effects of this type of transfer:

1. If you wish to sell or mortgage your property, it may be awkward because all of your children and their spouses must sign the deed or mortgage.
2. If any of your children have a judgment or tax lien, it may well attach to their remainder interest. This will usually mean that it must be satisfied before the property can be sold or mortgaged, resulting in a loss to your child. If a child later develops financial problems and files for bankruptcy, he or she will lose the remainder interest.
3. If any of your children have marital problems that end in divorce, remainder interest may figure in the property settlement and may pose a problem.
4. If the property is sold before you die, if there's a taxable gain, your children will have to pay income tax on a portion of the gain.
5. If the property is sold during your lifetime, your children will receive part of the sale proceeds and they will have no legal obligation to return any portion of it to you.
6. If you are receiving nursing care and the property is sold, a portion of the sale proceeds will be used to pay for your nursing care expense. The percentage is determined by published actuarial tables.
7. If any of your children die before you, it will be necessary to probate that child's interest. Usually, a remainder interest owned by a deceased child will go to his or her spouse. It will then require some special effort to have the surviving spouse transfer the property to grandchildren.

8. The property will be included in your taxable estate for estate tax purposes.
9. In the event of a sale of just your life estate or a sale by just one of your remaindermen, the term interest rule will apply. That means that no income tax basis is allowed on the sale and the entire sale price is treated as a taxable gain.
10. If, at a later time, you want your children to give back their remainder interest, the gift back will be regarded as a future interest and, therefore, part of their unified credit will be used up.

■ JOINT TENANCY ISSUES

Jointly owned property is probably the least understood area of estate planning, a topic we discussed in Chapter 4. People often refer to joint tenancy as the poor man's will. It can be useful in estate planning to put your property into joint tenancy with your spouse, child, parent, or another family member—if you know what you're doing.

Joint tenancy with right of survivorship means that each joint tenant has a full and undivided interest in the property. (The joint tenants are usually husband and wife, although they could also be business partners.) Bank accounts and real estate are the types of property most often held in joint tenancy.

Neither party can sell the property without the other's consent. The only exception to the rule is that either joint tenant can withdraw funds from a joint bank account. Upon death of a joint tenant, the entire property passes to the survivor(s) automatically, avoiding probate and the courts.

At least one advantage to owning property in a joint tenancy is that it avoids probate. But there are certain disadvantages to owning property in joint tenancy:

Unaffected by will. No joint tenant can transfer joint property by means of will instruction. A will distributes only property in an individual's name or an interest held in tenants-in-common. Since joint property transfers by right of survivorship, you can not control the disposition of joint property by will!

Undesired beneficiaries. Joint property may pass to someone you don't wish to receive it. Let's assume that a husband and a wife own all of their property jointly. If the husband dies first, his estate will automatically pass to his wife. Now the wife controls all of the property, and she can give it upon her death to whomever she wants—a new spouse, for example, and that spouse's children.

Incompetent spouse. The surviving spouse may not be experienced in money matters, or may be physically or mentally disabled. If this is the case, the survivor may well end up in probate for a living probate proceedings to determine who will act as conservator for that surviving spouse.

Estate tax issues. Since all joint property goes to the surviving spouse, it may be subject to estate tax when the surviving spouse dies. This is not a problem unless the surviving spouse's estate is larger than the amount of the unified credit/personal estate tax exemption. For 1999, the personal estate exemption is $650,000. However, it's very common with large estates for a husband and wife to do estate planning to minimize estate taxes, but forget to change the joint titling of their assets. This is done by having special provisions written into a will or trust that implements the credit shelter of the first spouse to die, thereby utilizing the personal estate exemption of both spouses. With joint tenancy ownership it does not work!

Income tax issues. Joint tenancy may create an income tax problem if the estate owns appreciated assets. If an individual purchased a parcel of real estate for $50,000 and at death it's worth $200,000, the surviving spouse who receives the real estate by means of a will can sell it for $200,000 and pay no capital gains tax. The income tax cost basis of the real estate is stepped up at death to the current market value that the real estate was valued at in the estate.

If the property was received through joint tenancy at death, the surviving joint tenant would be taxed on capital gains of $75,000. The basis in the property would be one-half of the purchase price of $50,000 ($25,000) plus a stepped up basis at death on the other one-half of the property ($100,000), which would equal $125,000. The selling price of $200,000 would create a $75,000 capital gain.

Unwanted family trouble. If an individual who transfers an asset to joint tenancy later decides that he or she wants it back, often unwanted family tensions are created. After the transfer of assets, the new joint tenant may not want to relinquish ownership in the asset. This could happen in a situation where a son or daughter is placed as joint tenant on a parent's asset. This situation can cause a stalemate and create problems that could well have been avoided. Jointly held bank accounts may be the most common cause of problems.

Many single people place bank accounts in joint tenancy with one or more of their children. Many elders feel that this is a simple strategy that allows a son or daughter to receive the money after death without any probate. However, if the child gets into a financial trouble (bankruptcy, divorce, or lawsuit), it may well prove disastrous for the parent, because one-half of the asset now belongs to that child and may be pursued by creditors.

There are better strategies, such as the Totten trust (as discussed in Chapter 6), annuities, and life insurance. You can also sidestep probate by establishing a living trust.

Joint tenancy is still the most common form of family ownership in America. It performs an important role in small estates. However, if you've accumulated wealth in excess of the personal estate exemption or you own and operate a business, you should develop a more advanced strategy in your estate plan.

SOMETHING FOR YOUR FUTURE HEIRS

Part of estate planning is preparing your future heirs. With that in mind, we suggest that you have them know a little about how to deal with the property they'll inherit from you. So, here's a little planning information for your heirs.

If you inherit property and then sell it, any capital gain means income tax. The tax is based on the amount of the gain, which is the difference between the sale price and the seller's basis. That cost basis is typically the original cost or investment in an asset, adjusted by such items as improvement or depreciation.

The cost basis of inherited property for the heir is the same as the value of that property as of the decedent's date of death or alternate valuation date. For appreciated property, the cost basis is stepped up to the property's fair market value when the property is inherited. When the property has declined in value, the cost basis steps down from its original cost to the lower current value.

Property jointly owned by spouses with right of survivorship is considered owned one-half by each. Therefore, only one-half of the total value of the property will qualify under the step-up in basis rule applied to inherited property.

One exception to the full step-up in value rules concerns appreciated property acquired by the decedent as a gift within one year of death. If the property passes from the decedent back to the person who gave it or that person's spouse, no step-up in cost basis will occur. The basis in the hands of the original donor or spouse will be the decedent's basis immediately before death.

The cost basis for appreciated property in an estate steps up to the fair market value for estate tax purposes. So, when the heir sells the property, only any gain in appreciation that occurred after the estate evaluation is taxable.

■ HOW TO EVALUATE A NURSING HOME

If you need to spend any time in a nursing home, long-term care facility, or nursing and rehabilitation center, you should choose carefully. To make a wise selection among the nursing homes in your area, use this checklist when you visit and research facilities.

Some of the questions are more important than others, of course, particularly in terms of your individual needs, both now and in the future. You probably will add questions to this list. The important point to remember is that you have a right to ask questions: choosing a health care facility is a big decision that requires a lot of information and some hard thinking.

You may also want to read the booklet provided by the Health Care Financing Administration, *HCFA Guide to Choosing a Nursing Home.* You may obtain a copy by calling the HCFA at 800-638-6833.

Licensing and Finances

______ Is the home licensed? (If so, ask to see the license.)

______ Does the administrator hold a current state license? (If so, ask to see it.)

______ Is the home approved for both Medicare and Medicaid?

______ What other insurance plans does the home accept?

______ What is included in the rate? (Get a written statement.)

______ What is not included in the rate?

______ Is a deposit required?

______ Are payment plans available?

Safety

______ When was the last state or local inspection, and what were the results?

______ Is the state inspection report available? (Be sure to review it.)

______ Is the home well lighted?

______ Are the rooms and the hallways free of clutter and other obstacles to walking or operating a wheelchair?

______ Are there handrails in the hallways?

______ Are there grab bars in the bathrooms?

______ Are hallways wide enough to allow two wheelchairs to pass easily?

______ Does the facility meet local, state, and federal fire codes?

______ Are all exits clearly marked, unobstructed, and easy to open?

______ Are evacuation plans visibly posted throughout?

______ How often does the staff hold fire drills?

______ Are there smoke detectors in the rooms and in hallways?

______ Are fire extinguishers easy to find and to use? Are they inspected annually?

______ Is there a sprinkler system?

______ Is there an emergency electric-power system?

______ Are stairway doors kept closed?

______ Are call buttons in rooms and baths easy to reach?

______ Is the inside of the home in good condition?

______ Do staff members clean up spills and other accidents quickly?

FIGURE 10B

Health care

- _______ Are there enough staff to appropriately care for residents?
- _______ How are residents' medical needs met?
- _______ Does the nursing home have an arrangement with a nearby hospital to handle emergencies?
- _______ Is the home near a cooperating hospital?
- _______ Is the home close enough to your physician?
- _______ Do residents get regular medical attention?
- _______ How often are residents seen by a doctor?
- _______ How often do doctors review medications?
- _______ What are the provisions for emergency medical care?
- _______ Are there arrangements for special services, such as dental, hearing, foot, and eye care?
- _______ Are drug services supervised by a certified pharmacist?
- _______ Does the facility employ a nursing supervisor?
- _______ Are RNs or LPNs on duty at all times?
- _______ Is a written nursing care policy available to residents? Is the policy enforced?
- _______ Do nurses and aides respond to calls promptly?
- _______ Is timely assistance available for incontinent residents?
- _______ Are nursing care records kept on each resident? Is there a physical therapy program directed by a qualified therapist?
- _______ Are services of speech and occupational therapists available?
- _______ Are mental health services available?
- _______ Are recommended exercise and therapy programs carried out? Does therapy cost extra? If so, how much?

Meals

- _______ Does a licensed dietitian on staff supervise the planning and preparation of meals?
- _______ Are meals varied, attractive, tasty, and served at appropriate temperatures? (Sample a meal if possible.)
- _______ Are meals served at appropriate intervals?
- _______ Is the dining room attractive, cheerful, and comfortable?

FIGURE 10B (CONTINUED)

_______ Is there enough time allowed for eating?

_______ Does the home provide for special diets?

_______ Does the staff help patients who need assistance with eating (at no extra charge)?

Atmosphere, Personal Space, and Visitors

_______ Is the facility free of unpleasant odors?

_______ Is it clean, comfortable, and cheerful?

_______ Are residents' rooms comfortable?

_______ Are residents allowed to decorate their rooms with personal articles?

_______ Are residents allowed to furnish rooms with their own furniture?

_______ Can residents have their own radios or televisions?

_______ Can a husband and a wife share a room?

_______ Are residents permitted to smoke in their rooms? If so, are they supervised?

_______ What are the rules regarding alcohol use?

_______ Are phones available for residents to make private phone calls?

_______ Are there restrictions on making or receiving phone calls?

_______ Is the home's environment homey rather than institutional?

_______ Do common areas and resident rooms contain comfortable furniture?

_______ Does the home have outdoor areas (patios, terraces, gardens, walkways, etc.) that residents can use freely?

_______ Is the home convenient for your family and friends to visit?

_______ What are visiting hours?

_______ Are there areas available for family members to visit privately?

Services

_______ Where does the home keep residents' money and other valuables?

_______ Are there provisions for personal banking services?

_______ Are there additional charges for personal laundry?

_______ Is there a store where residents can buy personal care items, stationery, postage stamps, and other sundries?

FIGURE 10B (CONTINUED)

Activities

_______ Is a social worker available to assist patients and their families?

_______ What types of social, cultural, educational, and recreational activities are available for residents? (Ask to see the schedule of activities.)

_______ Is the schedule of activities posted? (If not, why not?)

_______ Do scheduled activities take place?

_______ Are residents encouraged but not pushed to participate?

_______ Does the staff offer individual activities for residents who are confined to bed?

_______ Are there activity rooms and lounges?

_______ Are outside trips planned?

_______ Does the facility have contract with outside groups of volunteers?

_______ Are arrangements made to accommodate religious worship?

Interactions and Personal Rights

_______ Do interactions between staff members and residents seem warm and personal?

_______ Is there a written bill of rights for residents posted in plain view?

_______ Do staff members treat residents respectfully?

_______ Are staff members sensitive to the privacy and dignity of residents?

_______ Do staff members make an effort to meet the needs of each resident?

_______ Is there a resident council? If so, how often does it meet? What powers does it exercise?

_______ Is the facility free of discrimination in regard to race, sex, religion, or national origin?

_______ Are physical and chemical restraints used only under a doctor's orders?

_______ Is the use of restraints carefully monitored and reviewed?

_______ Do residents generally look contented and engaged?

_______ Are residents neatly groomed and appropriately dressed?

_______ Do staff members encourage residents to act independently?

FIGURE 10B (CONTINUED)

11 The Family-Owned Business: Structures, Strategies, and Succession

All of the chapters up to this point have focused on the individual, on personal financial matters in general. In this chapter, we turn to the particular concerns involved in owning a business.

As you know, a business can be owned in various ways, from a small sole proprietorship to a large publicly owned corporation. Each structure has its own unique inherent risks and rewards.

If you own a business, you're well aware of the risks of operating a business—competition, shortages of materials or labor, excess or inadequate production capacity, loss of important clients or customers, dramatic fluctuations in cash flow and prices, and changing economic conditions.

However, you may not be aware of the even greater risks that come with the form of the business you own. Whether your business is a sole proprietorship, a partnership, a closely held corporation, or a professional corporation, its structure poses certain risks that threaten the survival of your business and perhaps even the financial future of your family.

In the following three sections, we'll look at each type of business organization and discuss the risks that arise from the way each is structured.

■ Sole Proprietorships

A sole proprietorship is the easiest form of business to organize and to operate. There are no special legal requirements for either starting up or terminating a sole proprietorship. Because of the ease of starting and running this type of business, sole proprietorships are the most common form of business in the United States.

In addition to its simplicity, a sole proprietorship provides the flexibility to change the focus or the direction of a business. Since the business is owned by one individual, the owner is free in making business decisions.

The owner can determine what will happen to the business at retirement and, with proper planning, at death. The assets used in the business remain the personal property of the proprietor or his or her estate, instead of being titled in the name of the business, which would make it difficult for the business owner or heirs to get them back.

The Risks of Sole Proprietorship

The greatest risk that confronts a sole proprietorship may be the death of the proprietor. When the proprietor dies, in almost all cases the business dies as well. The business that has been the sole or primary source of income for the owner and family is worth little or nothing after the owner dies, except for any assets. The deceased owner's family is usually forced to liquidate the business at less than its actual value to pay estate settlement costs and taxes.

Since a sole proprietor's personal and business assets are usually one and the same, they both can be subject to attachment by the creditors of the business if the business gets into financial difficulty. The owner could lose all assets, personal as well as business.

Sole proprietorships also face problems of raising additional capital, since they can't bring in outside investors through issuing stocks and bonds. The proprietor must rely on funds generated by the business or borrowed from the bank, which inhibits the growth of the business. Selling or transferring a sole proprietorship can be difficult because the assets of the business usually have to be sold separately.

And when the proprietor dies, the executor of the estate must take possession of personal and business assets and pay personal and business debts.

■ PARTNERSHIPS

If two or more individuals find the sole proprietorship inadequate for the needs of their business but they don't want to go to the expense of setting up a corporation, the partnership may be the ideal compromise solution. A partnership is simply the association of two or more people who have agreed either verbally or in writing to combine their skills and resources for profit.

In a general partnership, each partner contributes a share of the capital and services to the business and has a share in the control, management, and liability of the business. Each partner is a principal in the business and has equal authority with the other partners and shares equally in the profits or losses, assuming that the partners have all made equal contributions to the business and they have not modified that equality by written agreement.

THE RISKS OF PARTNERSHIPS

The greatest risk of running a business as a general partnership is death: the death of a partner may dissolve a partnership automatically and instantaneously. The law requires that a partnership be dissolved upon the death of a 50% general partner—even if the partners have prepared agreements to the contrary.

The surviving partners could continue the business with or without a representative from the deceased partner's estate or family, but they would have to reorganize in the form of a new partnership. And the heirs of the deceased partner may be legally entitled to demand liquidation of the firm and division of the assets, if they choose.

Another risk in the general partnership form of business is the unlimited liability of all general partners for the debts of the partnership and any negligent acts of the other partners and employees. Each partner's personal assets are at risk for payment of the partnership liabilities.

■ CORPORATIONS

The corporate form of business grew out of a need to provide business with more stability and continuity than is found with the simpler forms of business organization. Although the variety of corporations has expanded to include closely held corporations, publicly owned corporations, C corporations, S corporations and Professional Corporations, they all share the following features:

- A corporation is a separate legal existence, independent of its owners, which means the business does not have to be dissolved upon the death of an owner.
- Ownership is evidenced by possession of stock, which entitles the owner to a proportionate share of profits and provides a vehicle for transferring ownership.
- The liability of each owner is limited to the amount of his or her investment.
- Management of daily affairs is by officers selected by the board of directors, who are elected by shareholders.
- Profits are distributed as dividends to stockholders.

Although all corporations share these characteristics, they can vary with respect to ownership, tax status, and the type of business conducted. These are the basic types of corporations:

- C Corporations—These are conventional corporations that pay tax directly to the IRS. They can be publicly owned or closely held. They are named C corporations after Subchapter C of the Internal Revenue Code.
- S Corporations—These are corporations that have elected to be taxed like partnerships. The corporation generally pays no tax; instead, all income and losses pass through directly to the stockholders, who pay taxes on their shares. These are named S corporations after Subchapter S of the Internal Revenue Code.
- Professional Corporations—These are corporations composed exclusively of professional service providers, such as doctors, lawyers, accountants, architects, and others licensed to practice a "learned profession" or provide a service. These corporations must file articles of incorporation with the state that meet the state's specific requirements.

C Corporation—A conventional corporation that pays tax directly to the IRS.

Closely held corporation—A corporation whose shares (or at least voting shares) are held by a single shareholder or closely-knit group of shareholders, who are generally active in the conduct of the business, which usually has no public investors. Also known as a close corporation.

Corporation—A corporation that generally pays no tax; all income and losses pass through directly to the stockholders, who pay taxes on their shares.

Professional Corporation—A corporation composed exclusively of doctors, lawyers, accountants, architects, and others licensed to practice a "learned profession" or provide a service.

The Risks of Incorporation

Incorporation eliminates or minimizes many of the risks inherent in a sole proprietorship or a partnership, such as liability for business obligations or the dissolution of a business at the death of an owner. However, it doesn't make the owners of a corporation—especially one that is closely held—immune to all misfortune.

The death of a major stockholder in a corporation can jeopardize the future of the business as well as the income and financial security of other shareholders.

When a stockholder in a closely held corporation dies without a business continuation plan, that situation naturally divides the shareholders into two groups with opposing priorities. On the one hand, the heirs and executor of the deceased shareholder will be concerned with immediate needs for income to pay estate settlement costs and provide for the family's financial needs. On the other hand, the surviving shareholders will be more concerned about long-term future and financial needs of the business.

The potential conflict arising from these opposing priorities is usually resolved by one of the following four alternative courses of action, each of which creates its own risks.

The surviving stockholders buyout the heirs of the deceased stockholder.

While this is the most logical solution to the problem, it can be the source of numerous problems. For example, will both parties be able to agree on a fair price for the deceased shareholder's stock? Can the surviving stockholders buy the stock immediately with cash or will they have to buy it on installment? In the latter case, are the heirs willing to wait?

The heirs enter the business as active stockholders.

Usually the heirs will be the decedent's spouse and children, who may or may not have the necessary experience to manage or significantly contribute to the success of the business. If the heirs are majority stockholders and lack knowledge of the business but insist on managing it, the future of the corporation may be in jeopardy.

The heirs enter the business as inactive stockholders.

Although potentially less damaging than the previous alternative, this option poses its own special problems. Since the heirs will need a source of income to replace that provided by the decedent, they may agree to stay out of the management of the business for a share of the profits. This idea may not appeal to the surviving stockholders, who then have to assume all responsibility for managing the company and pay out a large part of corporate profits as dividends to heirs who contribute nothing.

The heirs sell their stock to an outsider. This option again raises the issue of determining a fair price for the stock, assuming a buyer can be found. The surviving stockholders may have no control over to whom the stock can be sold or under what conditions it can be sold. If the deceased stockholder was a majority stockholder, selling his or her stock to an outsider would pass control of the business to a stranger, which could make the surviving stockholders' positions nearly untenable. What's to keep a leading competitor from buying the heirs' stock and taking over the business?

The essence of a corporation also can be put at risk by the departure or death of a key executive or employee, whether he or she is or is not a shareholder. Numerous studies have shown that the primary cause of business failure is a breakdown in management because of the loss of an experienced manager or key person. The loss of a key employee could disrupt the management of a corporation, reduce its earnings, affect the availability of credit, threaten customer relationships, create problems in finding a replacement, and/or jeopardize the loyalty and morale of other employees.

The risk that can result from the death or departure of a stockholder or key employee should make it obvious that the corporate form of business alone is no guarantee of stability and security for stockholders, regardless of whether they have minority or majority holdings.

The most valuable asset of any business is people. We've discussed the potentially devastating impact that the death or loss of an owner, partner, or other key person can have on a business—proprietorship, partnership, or corporation. The risks posed by a loss of control or the loss of a key employee can be minimized or even eliminated by advance planning using well-established business strategies.

■ BUSINESS CONTINUATION STRATEGIES

The operation of a business can be adversely affected by the death, disability, or departure of a co-owner or of a key person associated with the business. You can't prevent deaths, disabilities, or departures, but you can make plans to ensure that the business will continue.

Cross-Purchase Plans (a.k.a. Buy/Sell Agreements)

A cross-purchase plan may be the ideal solution for the problem of retaining control of your business after the death of a partner or co-owner. A cross-purchase or buy/sell agreement is a plan that provides for an orderly change of ownership when a business owner dies or becomes disabled.

This agreement is a legal contract signed by all of the owners of a business. If one of them dies, the others will buy the deceased's interests, which the estate must sell, at a specified price. In addition, each owner agrees not to dispose of his or her interest in the business without first offering it to the other owners at the previously agreed-upon price.

> *Cross-purchase agreement*—A contract that provides for an orderly transfer of ownership interests (stock or partnership interests) in a closely held business when an owner dies or becomes disabled. Also known as a buy/sell agreement.

The agreement serves the purposes of both the surviving business owners and the family of the deceased owner. It enables the remaining owners to acquire the interests of the late owner and ensure continuity of the business, while it provides the heirs of the deceased owner with fair and full payment for their interest in the business.

The only question is how the cross-purchase agreement should be funded. The surviving owners have four alternatives for funding their purchase of the interest:

Pay cash.

If the surviving owners have adequate personal assets outside the business, they can use accumulated capital for the purchase. However, if these assets are not liquid, the sudden forced transfer could result in substantial losses to the owners. Furthermore, using cash for this purchase will take away funds that could be used more profitably for business purposes.

Borrow the money.

The surviving owners may find it difficult, if not impossible, to borrow money after the loss of a key person because of questions about the viability of the business. Even if they succeed in borrowing the money, they would be mortgaging the future income of the business at the expense of profits and working capital.

Create a special savings fund.

The owners could make periodic deposits to a savings fund to accumulate the purchase price. However, one of the owners may die before the funding is completed, so there would still be a liquidity problem.

Use life insurance.

Each owner of the business could purchase life insurance policies on the other owners with face values equal to their interests in the business. In contrast to the disadvantages and uncertainties of the other methods, life insurance provides certainty and guarantees the effectiveness of the buy/sell agreement. By using life insurance to pay the purchase price, they pay out discounted dollars and will receive a federal income tax exclusion on the net gain when an owner's death matures the policy. (You may recall our discussion in Chapter 5 of using life insurance to fund estate liquidity.)

Stock Redemption (Entity) Plans

A cross-purchase plan can be impractical for a business with more than two or three owners, because of the number of insurance policies that would be necessary to cover all of the owners. A business with three owners would require six policies, for example, and a company with four owners would necessitate twelve policies.

Rather than buy that many policies, you could set up a stock redemption or entity plan. Under this plan, the corporation or partnership purchases the life insurance on each of the individual owners, becoming the policy owner and beneficiary.

Each policy would have a face value equal to the business interest of the insured, to ensure that adequate funds will be available to purchase the stock of any owner who might die. With such a plan, a business with four owners, for example, would need to purchase only four policies, rather than the twelve that would be required under a cross-purchase plan.

The Advantages of Buy/Sell Plans

There are benefits to buy/sell plans for everybody involved directly or indirectly with ownership of the business.

For the owners while living:

- A buy/sell plan establishes a guaranteed price and market for their interest in the business.
- They can feel assured that their heirs will receive full value.
- Cash values of the policy can provide funds for emergencies, opportunities, and retirement.

For the surviving owners:

- They retain control of the business.
- Creditors and employees are assured that the business will continue.
- Funds are guaranteed and provided when needed.
- Business credit is maintained and even strengthened.

For the heirs:

- They receive an immediate, fair price in cash.
- The estate can be settled promptly and efficiently.
- They are not burdened with business responsibilities.

Family Limited Partnership

Another type of ownership that has gained popularity is the family limited partnership.

A partnership could include parents, children, and grandchildren. The partners also could be entities such as trusts created for the benefit of the family members.

Forming a family limited partnership begins with an accurate assessment of the business and its value. Then there's paperwork (of course!) and a few critical decisions.

When organizing a family limited partnership, the most important decision for the family members may be whom to name as the general partner(s). The general partner(s) will have control over the partnership's business activities and determine how much of the partnership income is to be distributed to the partners.

Also, the general partner has unlimited liability in a family limited partnership. Newer forms of partnerships for tax purposes, limited liability companies, and limited liability partnerships may also allow a managing partner to have limited liability.

The family limited partnership can be an important tool when developing an estate preservation plan.

Typically the partnership allows structured management of business and investments. It also protects the family's assets from debt and creditors. The general partner can retain control of assets even after the transfer of ownership.

Often, a family limited partnership is established to allow the transfer of limited partnership interests from parents to children without transferring control. A family limited partnership ensures continuous ownership of a family business.

It also allows potential discounts for federal estate and gift tax on transfers of limited partnership interests. An estate planning strategy is to have the majority interest, owned by the individual with the highest net worth and his or her spouse, gradually gifted so that it is converted to a minority interest subject to discounts.

Discounts can be taken from the family limited partnership's value when minority and unmarketable interests are gifted to descendants. These discounts further reduce the value of the estate for estate and gift tax purposes.

Various discounts can be created:

- A lack of control discount is available for minority limited partnership interests. Because limited partners are not able to influence management decisions, the value of their interest is discounted to reflect this lack of control.
- A lack of marketability discount is available and reduces the value of privately held limited partnership interests that do not have a market for trading.

Situations in which a family limited partnership may be appropriate:

- To shift the income from a parent in a high tax bracket to a child in a lower tax bracket.
- To protect assets after a parent transfers partnership interests to younger generations when they otherwise may be lost due to poor management or divorce.
- To conduct a family business in a form other than a sole proprietorship.
- To provide flexibility in establishing rules for managing property.
- To simplify ownership and gifting of assets.
- To ease the distribution of assets at death among family members without having to remove the assets from the partnership.

Implementation of a succession plan for management and estate planning purposes is also very important. It can be achieved by choosing a non-managing general partner who will take over management after the general partner's interest is terminated.

LIMITED LIABILITY CORPORATIONS

A limited liability corporation is designed to attain one of the benefits enjoyed by stockholders of corporations, namely limited liability. Asset protection is a benefit of this form of operation. Also, the LLC has little ownership and operational restrictions.

Shareholders in an LLC are responsible for debts only up to their individual investment. The creditor, however, can request personal guarantees. The tax treatment and distribution rules of the limited liability corporation are complex and beyond the scope of our discussion here.

A limited liability company (LLC), however, is taxed as a partnership.

Losses incurred by the LLC pass through to owners (members) and are deductible under partnership rules.

An operating agreement that governs management is the fundamental element of the LLC. LLC voting privileges in most cases are directly related to the capital contributions of a member. Occasionally, with careful drafting, it also can be based on profit participation.

LLCs differ from limited partnerships in several ways. Limited partners of a limited partnership do not participate in management decisions. Members in a limited liability company may participate in management. General partners of a limited partnership participate in management and are liable for the debts.

The transfer of family business assets to family limited partnerships has become a common estate planning technique. An LLC can serve this purpose as effectively. Additionally, no family member has to perform as the general partner and assume liability or debts of the business.

SPECIAL LAND USE VALUATION: SECTION 2032A

There's a particular estate planning option that we should discuss here, because it affects a lot of family farms: Special Land Use Valuation, Internal Revenue Code Section 2032A. This is an alternative land valuation method used to calculate federal estate taxes.

Despite increasing awareness of this estate tax planning option, Section 2032A is generally misunderstood. It is widely perceived as easy, uncomplicated, and the primary method of solving farm estate planning problems.

Unfortunately, that perception often is based on a lack of accurate information concerning the complexities of 2032A and of its true advantages and disadvantages. Our purpose here is to examine Section 2032A and its potential role when being used to reduce estate taxes.

Essentially, the purpose of Section 2032A is to allow farmland to be valued as farmland. Quite simply, Section 2032A attempts to establish a productive value that is less than the farmland's fair market value (what it would bring if sold for its highest and best use). Valuing farmland at a lower price can save a significant amount of estate tax. Indeed, in select situations it can mean the difference between keeping a farm in the family or selling it to raise the cash to pay estate taxes.

For an estate to take advantage of Section 2032A, Special Land Use Valuation, it must meet the following conditions to qualify:

- The farm estate must be made up of "real property" used in farming that has a fair market value of at least 25% of the total value of the adjusted estate.
- The farm assets, both real and personal, must make up at least 50% of the estate.
- The farm real property must have been owned by the deceased or a family member for five of the previous eight years.
- The real property qualifying for special land use must pass to a qualifying heir (usually a family member).
- For five of the preceding eight years, the qualifying real property must have been farmed or there must have been material participation by the deceased or a member of the family.
- The executor (personal representative) must file an election for 2032A, with an agreement, signed by each person having an interest in the property, consenting to the liability for any estate tax recapture that may occur later.

(What's material participation? There's no definitive test, but physical work, participation in a substantial number of management decisions, and employment on a full-time basis are evidence of material participation.)

You might be wondering, "What does all that mean?" Let's look at an example.

Assume that your estate has a fair market value of $1 million—farmland valued at $250,000, equipment valued at $250,000, a house valued at $100,000, and personal property and investments valued at $400,000. Because your farmland constitutes 25% of your estate value and your equipment constitutes another 25%, your estate would meet both the 25% farm real estate and 50% farm assets rules.

But your estate would qualify only under the following three conditions:

- You owned the farmland and farmed it for five of the past eight years
- You transfer the farm to one or more of your children or other qualified family members who continue to farm the land or materially participate in the farming operation
- One of your heirs continues to farm or be materially engaged in the farming operation for another 10 years

Otherwise, any estate tax reduction is subject to recapture. If the qualifying farmland is taken out of production or sold to a non-family member during that 10-year period, there is a recapture of the estate tax reduction.

In essence, the special land use valuation creates a tax lien against your farm in favor of the U.S. Treasury. A negative aspect of this election is that it makes the qualifying heir personally liable for paying the additional estate tax.

How Section 2032A Reduces Estate Taxes

Section 2032A establishes an alternative value based on a formula. The value of the land is calculated as follows:

> the excess of the annual gross cash rental for comparable farmland in the same vicinity minus annual state and local real estate taxes (both determined on a five-year average) divided by the average annual effective interest rate of all new Federal Land Bank loans.

If cash rents in your area have averaged $100 for five years, real estate taxes have averaged $20 an acre, and the new average Federal Land Bank loan rate is 9.5%, we would calculate the value as follows:

($100 – $20) ÷ .095 = $842 per acre

This is the alternate value of your qualified land to calculate your estate taxes. The difference between using fair market value and 2032A special use value in calculating federal estate taxes becomes the amount of the lien that can be recaptured. If the Section 2032A special land election is made, the land does not receive a total step-up in income tax basis. The basis is adjusted only to the alternate special use value. This could have adverse income tax consequences later for your heir(s) if the land is sold within the 10-year period. If a recapture occurs, there is a step-up in basis to the extent of the recapture.

A significant planning consideration arises if you intend to have one or more of your children farm, yet you also have other, nonfarming children. You could have a situation where the farming children bear a greater share of the estate tax burden if a recapture occurs, because they are personally liable for taxes due at that time. Too often, the result is that the farming heirs have no choice but to have their non-active siblings as their partners for the 10-year period so they share the personal estate tax liability. To avoid unfair treatment of your heirs requires careful consideration.

Another unexpected burden may arise when, after the 2032A election has been successfully made, the farming heirs discover that the tax lien makes lenders uncomfortable with the new debt-to-equity margins. For the farming heir, restricted borrowing capabilities could very well make the difference between the farm succeeding and failing.

As farmers age and move into retirement, they often divest themselves of farm implements and equipment by gifting or selling to their farming children and not replacing these assets. This can create a potential imbalance when planning to use the 2032A valuation.

Over time, a retired farmer can reduce farm assets and increase nonfarm assets such as investments and savings. When farm assets are less than 50% of the adjusted gross estate, the estate no longer qualifies for the 2032A special land use election. Investing in more land seems attractive, but to qualify for Section 2032A the farmland must have been owned and farmed for five of the previous eight years. The strategy of buying more land also has a reduced impact in larger estates, because the valuation reduction cannot exceed $750,000.

So, if you believe that electing 2032A is simple and that it's the universal solution, you're mistaken. Electing 2032A involves complicated issues and many components to monitor over time to ensure that use of 2032A is consistent with your other estate plans. Here are several questions and issues to consider:

- Does your estate qualify for the 2032A election?
- Assuming that you live another 10 or 20 years, will your estate still qualify for the 2032A election?
- Could your heirs successfully operate under 2032A if it were elected today? What about in 10 or 20 years?
- Would restricted borrowing capabilities caused by the 2032A election significantly impact your farming heirs?
- Who would bear the burden of the potential 2032A recapture?
- Will your farming heirs want to be partners with your nonfarming heirs?
- Have you discussed these issues with your personal representative (executor), farming heirs, and estate planning attorney?
- Is the limited adjustment in income tax basis with the 2032A election a critical concern for your heirs?
- What other potential solutions should you explore?
- Is 2032A the best alternative for your estate and your heirs?

IRC Section 2032A has its place in farm estate planning. It can provide a viable alternative to other estate tax planning techniques. But it's important to understand that:

- There are potential pitfalls as well as benefits to using this election.
- There is no guarantee that a farm estate will qualify at the time the election is needed.

Many estate planners suggest that relying on the use of 2032A as the principal method to reduce estate taxes is not estate planning but rather the absence of it.

■ INSTALLMENT METHOD TO PAY ESTATE TAXES

Federal estate tax is payable in full within nine months of the date of death! But there's a break if the estate includes an interest in a closely held business. The Internal Revenue Code provides a limited alternative that allows an executor to pay a portion of the federal estate taxes over a period of years, under certain conditions.

Under Code Section 6166, the executor may elect to pay the federal estate tax allocated to the decedent's interest in a closely held business over a period of up to 14 years. During the first four years, interest is paid on the unpaid tax and interest. After that, annual installments of principal and interest are paid over as many as ten additional years.

Interest is payable at 2% on the deferred estate tax attributable to the first $1,000,000 of business value. (Unfortunately, although the Taxpayer Relief Act of 1997 reduced the interest rate and established a deduction for qualified family-owned businesses, as we discussed in Chapter 3, it also made the interest rate no longer deductible for either estate or income tax purposes.) The balance over that amount is charged a higher rate established by the IRS. This rate, based on the federal short-term rate plus 3%, changes every month. The first principal installment is due within four or five years of the date of death. Subsequent installments are to be paid at one-year increments.

Qualifying for Section 6166

How does an estate qualify for IRC Section 6166? There must be reasonable cause to qualify for the extension. Unfortunately, the IRS does not clearly define reasonable cause. It examines each situation on its own merits.

However, there are guidelines used to establish reasonable cause, including the following:

- The estate is unable to raise cash or sell off assets to pay the estate tax when due.
- The estate is made up of a large percentage of accounts receivable.
- The estate has insufficient liquidity to pay the estate tax and is restricted from otherwise borrowing against the estate assets and/or accelerating the collection of the accounts receivable.

Additionally, the gross estate must consist of an interest classified as a closely held business with a value in excess of 35% of the adjusted gross estate.

To qualify as a closely held business interest, the interest can be in a sole proprietorship, a partnership, or a corporation. Partnership interests qualify if at least 20% of the total capital interest in the partnership is included in the gross estate or if the partnership has fewer than 16 partners. Corporate stock qualifies if at least 20% of the voting stock is included in determining the gross estate of the decedent or if the corporation has fewer than 16 shareholders.

All active business assets are considered for the 35% of adjusted gross estate test. Only active business assets qualify for the deferred payment of estate taxes. Active means that the decedent actively managed the business.

The bottom line is that consideration should be given to using 6166 when the estate cannot pay the estate taxes without liquidating land, securities, and other assets or when the estate is earning a rate significantly higher than the interest expense on the 6166 installment method.

Let's close this chapter with an important question: Why shouldn't an estate rely on Section 6166 as an alternative to sound estate planning?

We have a lot of answers to that question. Section 6166 is not reliable. The percentage test may fail. Section 6166 only defers the liability to a later date. This may still be devastating to a business operation. Interest plus the tax increases the total cost to be paid. The money to pay the estate tax is still needed. It's more economical and usually easier to predetermine the source. Usually, only a small portion of the federal estate taxes will be deferred from current payment. The executor may remain personally liable for unpaid taxes during the 14 years and a federal tax lien will attach to the estate assets. Distributions to heirs from the estate may be delayed up to 14 years.

So, it's definitely wisest to do comprehensive estate planning—as we've advised throughout this book.

12 Ten Common Mistakes in Estate Planning

NO WILL OR ESTATE PLAN AT ALL. OBSOLETE WILLS.

When you don't have a will, your estate may be distributed according to the state's intestate succession rules. In essence, the state has a will for you. However, it may not distribute your property according to your wishes. The same fate could befall your estate if your will is an obsolete will or executed in another state.

LACK OF SPECIFIC DIRECTIONS IN YOUR WILL.

Many wills are drafted without provisions to deal with a family business, specific assets, or other issues that require more detailed attention in the will. This happens when standard distribution language is used in the will instead of detailed instructions for the proper distribution of complex assets.

JOINTLY OWNED PROPERTY WHEN THERE ARE SPECIFIC WILL INSTRUCTIONS.

If your will has specific instructions for specific property and you own that property in joint tenancy, the property will pass to the joint tenant(s) instead of being distributed according to the wishes you express in your will. Property in joint tenancy always passes to the other joint tenant(s).

JOINTLY OWNED PROPERTY WITH A-B TRUST PROVISIONS IN YOUR WILL.

If you use an estate tax reduction strategy in planning your estate and your will contains provisions for an A-B trust (credit shelter trust), joint tenant property will prevent your will from working properly. Property held in joint tenancy is not distributed by your will: it always passes to the other joint tenant(s).

A-B TRUST PROVISIONS WITH LARGE RETIREMENT PLANS.

Under the Employee Retirement Income Security Act of 1974 (ERISA), your spouse is the required beneficiary of your retirement plan — IRAs, 401(k)s, TSAs (tax-sheltered annuities), pensions, and profit-sharing plans. Unless you follow specific steps, this beneficiary requirement overrides your will. For your retirement plans to qualify for your personal estate exemption, pay special attention to naming your beneficiary.

PROPERTY OWNED IN TWO OR MORE STATES.

If you own property in a state other

than your state of domicile, you will have a second probate in that state to settle and transfer that real estate. One option to avoid any ancillary probate proceedings in another state is to put any real estate you own in that state into a trust.

IMPROPERLY OWNED LIFE INSURANCE TO PAY ESTATE TAXES.

If you've purchased life insurance to pay estate taxes and you own the policy on your own life, the death benefit is included in your gross estate to determine the amount of estate tax your estate will have to pay. One option that removes the death benefits from your taxable estate is a properly executed irrevocable life insurance trust.

UNDERVALUING OR NOT VALUING ASSETS WHEN DOING ESTATE PLANNING.

People quite often undervalue their assets. Consequently, when the estate is being settled, estate taxes may be greater than expected. This could have very adverse results if estate assets that should be preserved must be liquidated. When valuing assets, be realistic about their current value and expected growth. Don't forget to include any expected inheritance. This will help you plan appropriately for estate tax liability.

NO PROVISIONS MADE FOR MEDICAL EMERGENCIES.

Research has determined that one out of every two people will need some long-term care, and 40% of the people in this group are between the ages of 18 and 64. Causes for temporary disability or nursing home care are injuries, failing health, and illness. Estate planning should include a durable power of attorney or trust, a health care power of attorney, and a living will.

PROCRASTINATION.

An overdeveloped sense of longevity. Believing that there's plenty of time to do estate planning. Fear of mortality. These are three reasons why people often leave their estates in a mess to be sorted out by their heirs. Death and taxes—both are a certainty!

13 Glossary of Estate Planning Terms

A-B Trust—A common trust strategy created under a will to help maximize the unified credits and avoid estate taxes. By using it properly, a husband and wife can shelter $1,300,000 from estate taxes in 1999. By the year 2006, the combination can protect up to $2,000,000 from estate taxation. This strategy is also available through a living trust.

Ademption—The removal of property from an estate by the owner after he or she has bequeathed it in a will.

Adjusted Gross Income (AGI)—Your gross income reduced by certain adjustments.

Alternative Minimum Tax (AMT)—A tax that you may pay instead of income tax if you have tax preference items or certain deductions allowed in determining regular taxable income.

Annuity—Investment that pays a fixed amount to a designated beneficiary for a specified number of years or for life.

Artificially Administered Sustenance—Medical treatment consisting of giving special nutritional formulas, fluids, and/or medications through tubes when a person cannot drink and/or eat, to sustain life although it cannot reverse the dying process.

Attorney-in-Fact—Person to whom you give the authority to conduct all affairs, make decisions, and carry out financial tasks on your behalf through a power of attorney.

Beneficiary—An individual who receives benefits from an estate or from assets that have been placed in trust.

Brain Death—Condition in which the entire brain has stopped functioning, so the person is dead according to established medical criteria, but kept breathing with a respirator.

Buy/Sell Agreement—The most common way to transfer ownership of a business when a partner dies: all partners in a business agree to purchase the interest of any partner who dies. These agreements are often funded by life insurance. Also known as a cross-purchase agreement.

Bypass Trust—A trust that is set up to bypass the surviving spouse's estate, thereby allowing full use of the personal federal estate tax exemption for both spouses. Also known as the Credit Shelter, Family Trust, B Trust, or Family Credit Shelter Trust.

C Corporation—A conventional corporation that pays tax directly to the IRS. It may be publicly owned or closely held. (C corporations are named after Subchapter C of the Internal Revenue Code.)

Capital Gains Tax—The income tax that must be paid when appreciated assets are sold at a profit or when a depreciated asset is sold at more than its book value.

Cardiopulmonary Resuscitation (CPR)—A procedure used to restore breathing and a heartbeat, usually by applying pressure on the chest to keep blood flowing and sometimes by inserting a tube through the mouth or nose to get air into the lungs, connecting a ventilator to maintain breathing artificially, or using drugs or electrical shock to restart the heart.

Carrier—A private insurance company that contracts with the federal government to provide Medicare Part B coverage.

Charitable Remainder Trust (CRT)—A gift made in trust to a qualified charity, an arrangement that regularly pays income from the assets to the donor or another beneficiary during the donor's lifetime and then passes the remaining assets to the designated charity.

Codicil—A legal change to a will, written and properly witnessed.

Conservator—A person appointed by the court to be legally responsible for managing the financial affairs of a person who's incompetent, playing a role similar to that of a guardian.

Conservatorship—The management of financial and personal affairs for a person who has been declared legally incompetent by a court, which appoints a conservator for that purpose.

Consumer Price Index (CPI)—A federal measurement of inflation and deflation based on changes in the relative costs of goods and services for a typical consumer.

Contingent Beneficiary—Person named to succeed the grantor of a living will who has named himself or herself as beneficiary.

Contingent Trustee—Person named to succeed the grantor of a living will who has named himself or herself as trustee.

Credit Shelter Trust—A trust that reduces estate taxes by using the unified credits of both husband and wife and generates income for the surviving spouse. Also known as credit shelter family trust, family trust, bypass trust, B trust, family credit shelter trust, credit trust, and exemption trust.

Cross-Purchase Agreement—A contract that provides for an orderly transfer of ownership interests (stock or partnership interests) in a closely held business when an owner dies or becomes disabled. These agreements are often funded by life insurance. Also known as a buy/sell agreement.

Declarant—A person who makes a living will.

Declaration to Physicians—A form of living will, a document that specifies your wishes concerning health care treatment in the event that you are no longer able to make such decisions.

Devise—(as a noun) a bequest or gift in a will, (as a verb) to bequeath or give in a will.

Dialysis—Medical treatment used to remove waste products from the blood when the kidneys fail to work properly.

Disclaimer—A formal legal refusal by a person to accept property willed to him or her. The property then passes to the next person in the line of succession.

Do Not Resuscitate (DNR)—A physician's order that, in the event of a sudden cardiac or respiratory arrest, no cardiopulmonary resuscitation (CPR) will be initiated, although all other medical and nursing care will continue.

Durable Power of Attorney—A written document by which a person designates another person to act on his or her behalf. It is not terminated by subsequent disability or incapacity of the principal.

Durable Power of Attorney for Health Care—A written document by which a person designates another person to act on his or her behalf to make health care decisions if he or she is unable to do so.

Estate—All the assets owned by an individual at death, including home, real estate, bank accounts, securities, retirement plans, life insurance, etc.

Estate Liquidity—The extent to which an estate consists of cash or assets that can be easily converted to cash with little or no loss of value.

Estate Planning—Planning for management of assets during life and for orderly distribution of assets at death to heirs with the least possible delay and cost.

Estate Tax—A transfer tax imposed on the fair market value of property left at death; often called an inheritance tax or a death tax.

Executor—The person or institution named in a will to be responsible for the management of the assets and the ultimate transfer of the property; also commonly called a personal representative.

Fiscal Intermediary—A private insurance company that contracts with the federal government to provide Medicare Part A coverage.

Generation-Skipping Transfer Tax—A tax levied on assets that are transferred directly to grandchildren or lower generations. Each person has a $1,000,000 exemption from the GST tax.

Generation-Skipping Transfer—The passing of assets from the owner to his or her grandchildren, so that they are never in the possession of the owner's child or children.

Generation-Skipping Trust—A trust that allows assets to bypass a generation, so that grandchildren receive property directly from their grandparents, without it passing through their parents.

Gift—Any voluntary transfer of property or property interests to another without adequate consideration.

Gift Tax—A tax imposed on transfers of property by gift that exceeds the annual gift exclusion allowance, currently $10,000 per recipient per year.

Grantor—The person who sets up the trust, names the beneficiary and the trustee, and transfers the assets to the trust.

Guardian—A person who's legally responsible for managing the affairs and the care of a minor or a person who's incompetent; in some states a conservator plays a similar but more limited role.

Health-Care Proxy—A durable power of attorney for health care that appoints an agent to make decisions about medical treatment for the principal.

Heir—Person who inherits property when somebody dies.

Incapacitation—In general, the loss of mental competence, the inability to make decisions.

Individual Retirement Arrangement (IRA)—A financial construct that allows you to contribute to an interest-earning account for a specific purpose, originally retirement but now education as well (popularly known as Individual Retirement Account).

Insurance Trust—Irrevocable Life Insurance Trust (ILIT). A type of irrevocable trust used to maintain a life insurance contract outside of an estate. Typically used to provide estate liquidity and/or to pay estate taxes and settlement costs.

Intestate—The state of dying without a will. Assets are then distributed through the probate process and according to the state's will for an individual.

Intestate Succession—The process for determining what will happen to the property and any minor children of a person who dies without a will (intestate).

Irrevocable Life Insurance Trust (ILIT)—A trust that owns a life insurance policy, so that death benefit proceeds do not enter the estate and get taxed.

Irrevocable Trust—A trust that the trustor (grantor) cannot revoke or change.

Joint Tenancy—A form of ownership that provides for distribution of an interest at death to the other joint tenant(s). Joint tenant property is not transferable by will. Joint tenancy avoids probate.

Joint Tenants in Common—Owners of a shared asset, with the interest of any owner, upon death, becoming part of that person's estate.

Joint Tenants with Rights of Survivorship—Owners of a shared asset, with the interest of any owner, upon death, passing to the surviving co-owners.

Letter of Instructions—A memo that contains such information as the location of your will, the location of other vital documents, and any wishes for your funeral and burial.

Life Estate—A type of ownership that splits an asset into two parts: full benefit during life for the owner or life tenant and the remaining interest passing directly to heirs (remaindermen).

Life Tenant—A person who makes a lifetime transfer of a property and retains all use of the property until death, at which time it passes to the remainderman.

Life-Sustaining Treatment—Medical treatment that allows life to continue, although it cannot cure or reverse the patient's condition.

Liquidity—The degree to which an asset can be converted into cash quickly and with little or no loss of value.

Living Probate—The court-supervised process of managing the assets of one who is incapacitated.

Living Trust—A trust that a person creates during his or her lifetime to manage assets and ultimately distribute them upon incapacity or after death.

Living Will—A document in which a person specifies the kind and extent of medical care he or she wants in the event that he or she becomes terminally ill and incapable of expressing his or her wishes.

Long-Term Care Insurance (LTCI)—Private insurance to cover the high costs of long-term care (also called custodial care) for people with chronic health conditions and/or physical disabilities who are unable to care for themselves.

Look-Back Period—A waiting period before a Medicaid application is filed or the applicant enters a nursing home.

Marginal Tax—The tax imposed on an estate that is valued in excess of the unified credit exemption, when the value of lifetime gifts has been included.

Medicaid—A joint federal/state program that provides medical care to the needy; the federal government sets minimum standards that all state Medicaid programs must meet and then each state decides how much its programs will cover.

Medicare—A federal health insurance program primarily for people over age 65 who are receiving Social Security retirement benefits.

Medigap—Health insurance policies that supplement Medicare coverage.

Ordering Rules—Procedure for determining the status of withdrawals from Roth IRAs, as established by the Tax Technical Corrections Act of 1998.

Per Capita—Distribution that divides property equally among a group of named beneficiaries, regardless of their degree of kinship to the decedent. Example: a daughter, a grandson, an aunt, and a great nephew would all take equal shares if they were in the designated per capita class.

Per Stirpes—Distribution by line of descent, with any children of a deceased beneficiary splitting his or her share equally. ("Per stirpes" is a Latin term meaning by lineage.)

Personal Exemption—The amount of estate assets exempt from federal estate taxes. In 1999, the exemption is $650,000 using the Unified Tax Credit of $211,300. The personal exemption will increase to $1,000,000 in the year 2006.

POD (Payable-on-Death) Accounts—A form of ownership to name a beneficiary on a bank or financial institution account, typically used in lieu of joint ownership. Also known as a Totten trust.

Pour-over Will—A will or a provision in a will that directs property to go to another legal entity, usually a trust.

Power of Attorney—Written authorization enabling a person to designate another person to act on his behalf.

Present Interest—The right to use a gift immediately.

Probate—The legal procedure to determine, if there's a will, whether the will is valid or, if there's no will, how the estate should be distributed.

Professional Corporation—A corporation composed exclusively of professional service providers, such as doctors, lawyers, accountants, architects, and others licensed to practice a "learned profession" or provide a service. It must file articles of incorporation with the state that meet the state's specific requirements.

Proxy (Health Care)—A person designated in the living will to make health care decisions for the declarant or principal when he or she can no longer do so.

Qualified Terminal (or Terminable) Interest Property (QTIP) trust—A trust that uses the marital deduction at estate settlement and allows the grantor to determine to whom the trust assets will pass when the surviving spouse dies. The trust income must be paid to the surviving spouse and no person(s) can have the right to appoint the property to anyone other than the spouse during his or her life.

Reasonable Medical Practice—Practice that meets standards of care established by experience and provides reasonable expectation of benefit for a particular patient in a particular situation and in accordance with state law and organizational policy.

Remainderman—A person who has a future interest in a life estate or a trust.

Residuary Estate—What remains of an estate after all specific property bequests have been made.

Respirator/Ventilator—A machine that helps a person breathe or that substitutes for natural breathing when a person is unable to breathe because of illness or injury. Use of a respirator or a ventilator requires insertion of a tube through the nose or mouth or a tracheostomy (a surgical opening in the throat).

Retitle—To change legal ownership of an asset; the usual types of ownership are individual, joint tenancy, or tenancy in common.

Roth IRA—Individual Retirement Arrangement created by the Taxpayer Relief Act of 1997 that differs from the traditional IRA in that contributions are not tax-deductible but withdrawals are tax-free.

S Corporation—A corporation that is taxed like a partnership. The corporation generally pays no tax; instead, all income and losses pass through directly to the stockholders, who pay taxes on their shares. (S corporations are named after Subchapter S of the Internal Revenue Code.)

Simplified Employee Pension (SEP)—A simple, inexpensive pension plan designed for small business owners and self-employed individuals as an alternative to the 401(k), profit sharing, and pension plans.

Special Needs Trust—A legal arrangement that allows a person to provide for a disabled loved one without interfering with government benefits.

Stepped-up Basis—For income tax purposes, the cost basis establishes the level over which capital gain on sale is assessed. Assets that are gifted to heirs during lifetime carry their original cost basis when transferred. Assets gifted at death receive a stepped-up cost basis to the market value for estate tax purposes.

Survivorship Life Insurance—A life insurance policy that covers two people, usually spouses, and pays off only when the second person dies. Also known as joint, joint survivorship, two-life, or second-to-die.

Taxable Estate—The amount, after adjustments, of an estate value that is subject to federal estate tax.

Tenants in Common—A form of ownership that provides for collective ownership of undivided shares of an asset whereas the interest is transferable by will.

Terminal Condition—An incurable or irreversible condition in which any medical treatment will only prolong the dying process.

Testamentary Trust—A trust set up in a will and funded at death.

Testate—The state of dying with a valid will.

Testator/Testatrix—The man or woman who makes out a will and whose estate is to be distributed.

Title/Titling—Ownership of an asset, usually as individual owner, joint tenants, or tenants in common.

Totten Trust—A form of ownership to name a beneficiary on a bank or financial institution account, typically used in lieu of joint ownership. The shared account belongs to the depositor until he or she dies, then passes to the designated beneficiary. Also known as a payable-on-death (or pay-on-death) or POD account, informal trust, or bank trust account.

Transfer Tax—A tax imposed when ownership of property passes from one person to another, as a gift or through a will.

Trust—A legal arrangement under which a person, or persons, or institution controls property for the benefit of the trust beneficiaries. The three parties to a trust include: the one who transfers property (trustor, grantor), the manager (trustee), and the beneficiaries. In the case of Living Trusts, the trustor, trustee and beneficiaries are usually the same individual(s).

Trustee—The individual or institution responsible for managing a trust.

Trustor—The individual who creates and transfers assets to a trust. Also known as grantor.

Unified Credit—A credit the federal government gives each individual to use against federal estate taxes and excess gifts transferred during lifetime. The credit is $211,300 in 1999 and will rise incrementally to $345,800 in 2006, which is equivalent to a $1,000,000 exemption.

Uniform Gifts to Minors Act (UGMA) account—An account set up for a minor, with an adult designated as custodian of the property. The minor is the legal owner of the property, pays taxes on earnings generated by the property, and has an unrestricted right to use it upon reaching the age of majority (18 to 21, depending on the state).

Uniform Transfers to Minors Act (UTMA) account—The same as Uniform Gifts to Minors Act (UGMA) account.

Unlimited Marital Deduction—An individual can pass an entire estate regardless of size to a surviving spouse, without estate or gift taxes.

Vegetative State—A state in which a person is unable to talk or think or understand others. This condition, which can result from strokes and other diseases of the brain, is irreversible except in rare circumstances. A person in this state needs support in all aspects of care.

Wealth Replacement Trust—A trust set up to compensate heirs for a contribution to charity of assets that would otherwise have been included in the estate for the heirs.

Will—A legal document that is put into effect at the death of an individual. It serves as a list of instructions to the probate court on how estate assets should be distributed absent a joint owner or beneficiary designation.

Asset Inventory and Estate Planning Worksheet

	Present Value	Growth Rate	Value 10 Years	Value 20 Years
Cash Assets				
Checking				
Savings				
Money Market				
C.D.'s				
C.D.'s				
Other				
Investments				
Mutual Funds				
Corporate Bonds				
Tax-exempt Bonds				
Corporate Stocks				
Annuities				
Limited Partnerships				
Keogh				
SEP				
IRA				
IRA				
Life Insurance				
Life Insurance				
Use Assets & Real Estate				
Land				
Land				
Business Assets				
Tangible Property				
Inventory				
Commodities				
Livestock				
Closely Held Stocks				
Personal Residence				
Other				
Other				
Total Assets				
Outstanding Debt				
Land Debt				
Real Property Debt				
Residence Debt				
Equipment Debt				
Personal Debt				
Total Debt				
Net Estate				

Allocation of Ownership

	Present Value	Husband	Wife	Joint Tenancy	Tenants in Common
Cash Assets					
Checking					
Savings					
Money Market					
C.D.'s					
C.D.'s					
Other					
Investments					
Mutual Funds					
Corporate Bonds					
Tax-exempt Bonds					
Corporate Stocks					
Annuities					
Limited Partnerships					
Keogh					
SEP					
IRA					
IRA					
Life Insurance					
Life Insurance					
Use Assets & Real Estate					
Land					
Land					
Business Assets					
Tangible Property					
Inventory					
Commodities					
Livestock					
Closely Held Stocks					
Personal Residence					
Other					
Other					
Total Assets					
Outstanding Debt					
Land Debt					
Real Property Debt					
Residence Debt					
Equipment Debt					
Personal Debt					
Total Debt					
Net Estate					

Roth IRA Dist.

Lump Sum Amount Of IRA	Distribution Amount Annually	Annual Rate Of Return	15.00% Roth IRA Account	28.00% Roth IRA Account	31.00% Roth IRA Account	36.00% Roth IRA Account	39.60% Roth IRA Account
$973,704	$103,973.55	10.00%	$827,648	$701,067	$671,855	$623,170	$588,117
			($88,377.48)	($74,860.97)	($71,741.67)	($66,543.01)	($62,800.00)

Years	Distribution	0.00% After Tax Amount	15.00% After Tax Amount	28.00% After Tax Amount	31.00% After Tax Amount	36.00% After Tax Amount	39.60% After Tax Amount
1	$103,973.55	$103,973.55	$88,377.52	$74,860.96	$71,741.75	$66,543.07	$62,800.03
2	$103,973.55	$103,973.55	$88,377.52	$74,860.96	$71,741.75	$66,543.07	$62,800.03
3	$103,973.55	$103,973.55	$88,377.52	$74,860.96	$71,741.75	$66,543.07	$62,800.03
4	$103,973.55	$103,973.55	$88,377.52	$74,860.96	$71,741.75	$66,543.07	$62,800.03
5	$103,973.55	$103,973.55	$88,377.52	$74,860.96	$71,741.75	$66,543.07	$62,800.03
6	$103,973.55	$103,973.55	$88,377.52	$74,860.96	$71,741.75	$66,543.07	$62,800.03
7	$103,973.55	$103,973.55	$88,377.52	$74,860.96	$71,741.75	$66,543.07	$62,800.03
8	$103,973.55	$103,973.55	$88,377.52	$74,860.96	$71,741.75	$66,543.07	$62,800.03
9	$103,973.55	$103,973.55	$88,377.52	$74,860.96	$71,741.75	$66,543.07	$62,800.03
10	$103,973.55	$103,973.55	$88,377.52	$74,860.96	$71,741.75	$66,543.07	$62,800.03
11	$103,973.55	$103,973.55	$88,377.52	$74,860.96	$71,741.75	$66,543.07	$62,800.03
12	$103,973.55	$103,973.55	$88,377.52	$74,860.96	$71,741.75	$66,543.07	$62,800.03
13	$103,973.55	$103,973.55	$88,377.52	$74,860.96	$71,741.75	$66,543.07	$62,800.03
14	$103,973.55	$103,973.55	$88,377.52	$74,860.96	$71,741.75	$66,543.07	$62,800.03
15	$103,973.55	$103,973.55	$88,377.52	$74,860.96	$71,741.75	$66,543.07	$62,800.03
16	$103,973.55	$103,973.55	$88,377.52	$74,860.96	$71,741.75	$66,543.07	$62,800.03
17	$103,973.55	$103,973.55	$88,377.52	$74,860.96	$71,741.75	$66,543.07	$62,800.03
18	$103,973.55	$103,973.55	$88,377.52	$74,860.96	$71,741.75	$66,543.07	$62,800.03
19	$103,973.55	$103,973.55	$88,377.52	$74,860.96	$71,741.75	$66,543.07	$62,800.03
20	$103,973.55	$103,973.55	$88,377.52	$74,860.96	$71,741.75	$66,543.07	$62,800.03

Years	Annual Contribution	10.00% Growth Rate	15.00% Net Roth IRA	10.00% Growth Rate	28.00% Net Roth IRA	10.00% Growth Rate	31.00% Net Roth IRA	10.00% Growth Rate	36.00% Net Roth IRA	10.00% Growth Rate	39.60% Net Roth IRA	10.00% Growth Rate
1	$2,000	$2,200	$1,700	$1,870	$1,440	$1,584	$1,380	$1,518	$1,280	$1,408	$1,208	$1,329
2	$2,000	$4,620	$1,700	$3,927	$1,440	$3,326	$1,380	$3,188	$1,280	$2,957	$1,208	$2,790
3	$2,000	$7,282	$1,700	$6,190	$1,440	$5,243	$1,380	$5,025	$1,280	$4,660	$1,208	$4,398
4	$2,000	$10,210	$1,700	$8,679	$1,440	$7,351	$1,380	$7,045	$1,280	$6,535	$1,208	$6,167
5	$2,000	$13,431	$1,700	$11,417	$1,440	$9,670	$1,380	$9,268	$1,280	$8,596	$1,208	$8,112
6	$2,000	$16,974	$1,700	$14,428	$1,440	$12,222	$1,380	$11,712	$1,280	$10,864	$1,208	$10,253
7	$2,000	$20,872	$1,700	$17,741	$1,440	$15,028	$1,380	$14,402	$1,280	$13,358	$1,208	$12,607
8	$2,000	$25,159	$1,700	$21,385	$1,440	$18,114	$1,380	$17,360	$1,280	$16,102	$1,208	$15,196
9	$2,000	$29,875	$1,700	$25,394	$1,440	$21,510	$1,380	$20,614	$1,280	$19,120	$1,208	$18,044
10	$2,000	$35,062	$1,700	$29,803	$1,440	$25,245	$1,380	$24,193	$1,280	$22,440	$1,208	$21,178
11	$2,000	$40,769	$1,700	$34,653	$1,440	$29,353	$1,380	$28,130	$1,280	$26,092	$1,208	$24,624
12	$2,000	$47,045	$1,700	$39,989	$1,440	$33,873	$1,380	$32,461	$1,280	$30,109	$1,208	$28,415
13	$2,000	$53,950	$1,700	$45,857	$1,440	$38,844	$1,380	$37,225	$1,280	$34,528	$1,208	$32,586
14	$2,000	$61,545	$1,700	$52,313	$1,440	$44,312	$1,380	$42,466	$1,280	$39,389	$1,208	$37,173
15	$2,000	$69,899	$1,700	$59,415	$1,440	$50,328	$1,380	$48,231	$1,280	$44,736	$1,208	$42,219
16	$2,000	$79,089	$1,700	$67,226	$1,440	$56,944	$1,380	$54,572	$1,280	$50,617	$1,208	$47,770
17	$2,000	$89,198	$1,700	$75,819	$1,440	$64,223	$1,380	$61,547	$1,280	$57,087	$1,208	$53,876
18	$2,000	$100,318	$1,700	$85,270	$1,440	$72,229	$1,380	$69,220	$1,280	$64,204	$1,208	$60,592
19	$2,000	$112,550	$1,700	$95,667	$1,440	$81,036	$1,380	$77,659	$1,280	$72,032	$1,208	$67,980
20	$2,000	$126,005	$1,700	$107,104	$1,440	$90,724	$1,380	$86,943	$1,280	$80,643	$1,208	$76,107

Years	Annual Contribution	10.00% Growth Rate	15.00% Net Roth IRA	10.00% Growth Rate	28.00% Net Roth IRA	10.00% Growth Rate	31.00% Net Roth IRA	10.00% Growth Rate	36.00% Net Roth IRA	10.00% Growth Rate	39.60% Net Roth IRA	10.00% Growth Rate
21	$2,000	$140,805	$1,700	$119,685	$1,440	$101,380	$1,380	$97,156	$1,280	$90,116	$1,208	$85,047
22	$2,000	$157,086	$1,700	$133,523	$1,440	$113,102	$1,380	$108,389	$1,280	$100,535	$1,208	$94,880
23	$2,000	$174,995	$1,700	$148,745	$1,440	$125,996	$1,380	$120,746	$1,280	$111,997	$1,208	$105,697
24	$2,000	$194,694	$1,700	$165,490	$1,440	$140,180	$1,380	$134,339	$1,280	$124,604	$1,208	$117,595
25	$2,000	$216,364	$1,700	$183,909	$1,440	$155,782	$1,380	$149,291	$1,280	$138,473	$1,208	$130,684
26	$2,000	$240,200	$1,700	$204,170	$1,440	$172,944	$1,380	$165,738	$1,280	$153,728	$1,208	$145,081
27	$2,000	$266,420	$1,700	$226,457	$1,440	$191,822	$1,380	$183,830	$1,280	$170,509	$1,208	$160,918
28	$2,000	$295,262	$1,700	$250,973	$1,440	$212,589	$1,380	$203,731	$1,280	$188,968	$1,208	$178,338
29	$2,000	$326,988	$1,700	$277,940	$1,440	$235,431	$1,380	$225,622	$1,280	$209,272	$1,208	$197,501
30	$2,000	$361,887	$1,700	$307,604	$1,440	$260,559	$1,380	$249,702	$1,280	$231,608	$1,208	$218,580
31	$2,000	$400,276	$1,700	$340,234	$1,440	$288,198	$1,380	$276,190	$1,280	$256,176	$1,208	$241,766
32	$2,000	$442,503	$1,700	$376,128	$1,440	$318,602	$1,380	$305,327	$1,280	$283,202	$1,208	$267,272
33	$2,000	$488,953	$1,700	$415,610	$1,440	$352,046	$1,380	$337,378	$1,280	$312,930	$1,208	$295,328
34	$2,000	$540,049	$1,700	$459,041	$1,440	$388,835	$1,380	$372,634	$1,280	$345,631	$1,208	$326,189
35	$2,000	$596,254	$1,700	$506,816	$1,440	$429,303	$1,380	$411,415	$1,280	$381,602	$1,208	$360,137
36	$2,000	$658,079	$1,700	$559,367	$1,440	$473,817	$1,380	$454,074	$1,280	$421,171	$1,208	$397,480
37	$2,000	$726,087	$1,700	$617,174	$1,440	$522,783	$1,380	$501,000	$1,280	$464,696	$1,208	$438,556
38	$2,000	$800,896	$1,700	$680,761	$1,440	$576,645	$1,380	$552,618	$1,280	$512,573	$1,208	$483,741
39	$2,000	$883,185	$1,700	$750,707	$1,440	$635,893	$1,380	$609,398	$1,280	$565,238	$1,208	$533,444
40	$2,000	$973,704	$1,700	$827,648	$1,440	$701,067	$1,380	$671,855	$1,280	$623,170	$1,208	$588,117